FOSTERING
STUDENT SUCCESS

ALA Editions purchases fund advocacy, awareness, and accreditation programs for library professionals worldwide.

FOSTERING STUDENT SUCCESS

Academic, Social, and Financial Initiatives

EDITED BY SIGRID KELSEY

CHICAGO 2022

© 2022 by the American Library Association

Extensive effort has gone into ensuring the reliability of the information in this book; however, the publisher makes no warranty, express or implied, with respect to the material contained herein.

ISBN: 978-0-8389-3829-4 (paper)

Library of Congress Cataloging-in-Publication Data

Names: Kelsey, Sigrid, editor.
Title: Fostering student success : academic, social, and financial initiatives / edited by Sigrid Kelsey.
Description: Chicago : ALA Editions, 2022. | Includes bibliographical references and index. | Summary: "In this book, academic librarians examine how their libraries are responding to the changing needs of students to provide support in key areas such as advancing the quality of learning, fostering inclusion, and driving down costs"—Provided by publisher.
Identifiers: LCCN 2021051389 | ISBN 9780838938294 (paperback)
Subjects: LCSH: Academic libraries—United States—Relations with faculty and curriculum. | Academic libraries—United States—Relations with faculty and curriculum—Case studies. | Academic libraries—United States—Services to minorities. | Libraries and public health—United States. | COVID-19 Pandemic, 2020—United States.
Classification: LCC Z675.U5 F685 2022 | DDC 027.70973—dc23/eng/20211216
LC record available at https://lccn.loc.gov/2021051389

Book design by Kim Hudgins in the Source Sans and Source Serif typefaces. Cover images © Adobe Stock.

♾ This paper meets the requirements of ANSI/NISO Z39.48-1992 (Permanence of Paper).

Printed in the United States of America

26 25 24 23 22   5 4 3 2 1

Contents

Introduction ...ix

PART I   SUPPORT IN RAPIDLY CHANGING LEARNING ENVIRONMENTS

1. Taking a Byte Out of the Data Divide ...3
How an Academic Library Made Data Skills More Accessible by Creating a Makerspace
JOYCE GARCZYNSKI

2. Small Victories in STEM Librarianship ... 13
Taking on the Big Problem of Missing Information Literacy Instruction in Science Curricula and the Case of First-Generation Students
ELIZABETH PICKARD AND MICHELLE R. DESILETS

3. Identifying and Addressing the Evolving Accessibility Limitations of Rural Community College Students ... 27
HEATHER VANDYNE AND RACHEL KOSZALKA

4. Together from the Ground Up ... 37
Deconstructing the Research Process for First-Semester Students at Louisiana State University
SARAH SIMMS, NARCISSA HASKINS, AND EBONY MCDONALD

5. So Close and Yet So Remote ... 51
Using Technologies to Provide High-Touch, Personalized Support for Vulnerable Students
ROSALIND FIELDER-GISCOMBE AND GABRIELLE TOTH

vi / CONTENTS

6 Reenvisioning Learning in a Time of Disruption 61
JENNIFER MATTHEWS AND DEBORAH GASPAR

PART II **PROGRAMMING THAT FOSTERS INCLUSION**

7 Information Privilege and First-Generation Students.................. 71
A Librarian-in-Residence Program to Facilitate Information Access at the University of Wyoming
KRISTINA CLEMENT

8 Aflame and Unafraid 81
A Case Study on Creating Interactive Programming in Remote Learning
KARINA KLETSCHER AND JENNIFER TIRRELL

9 Inclusive Programming........... 93
Empathy, Support, and Access as Foundational Tools
TARIANA SMITH

10 Student Well-Being and Libraries 103
Addressing Systemic Racism and COVID-19
JASON COLEMAN, LIS PANKL, AND LEO S. LO

11 Employing the Disenfranchised Student for Mentoring and Empowerment 115
MICHELLE REALE

PART III LIBRARIES PROVIDING FINANCIAL SUPPORT

12 Loving Libraries 125
Stanford University Library's Paid Summer Internships
FELICIA A. SMITH

13 Throwing the University Wide Open 135
Textbook Affordability and COVID-19
ZARA WILKINSON

14 Bridging the Digital Divide in Appalachia 149
Lending Technology with a Personal Librarian
JONATHAN ROY WILSON

15 Laptops for Students 159
An Academic and Public Library Partnership
SHANNON L. DEW, GRETCHEN MITCHELL, AND SUSAN B. MYTHEN

16 Paid Positions for Students 171
A Win-Win for Everyone Involved
PAIZHA STOOTHOFF

About the Editor and Contributors ... 183

Index ... 191

BY SIGRID KELSEY

Introduction

While libraries have traditionally supported student learning, engaged in programming around social issues, and provided resources to allay educational costs, the ways in which libraries are meeting these needs are evolving in response to rapid changes brought about by current events like the pandemic, racial justice movements, and changing student demographics. These current events have magnified students' needs in significant ways.

About 37 percent of college students are over the age of 25, and of these, nearly 66 percent of them work, with 25 percent of them parenting. The proportion of white college students is decreasing, and universities are recruiting more nontraditional students due to the drop in population among high school-aged prospective students. About 31 percent of college students live at or beneath the federal poverty level.[1] The impacts of the coronavirus will expand the populations of students in financial need for years to come.

In this book, academic librarians examine how their libraries are responding to the changing needs of students to provide support in key areas such as advancing the quality of learning, fostering inclusion, and driving down costs.

Many of the chapters have a special focus on supporting the success of students who are members of what the current literature is calling "vulnerable" groups. Vulnerable students are those who face barriers or challenges that can impede their success in school: financial insecurity, racism, childcare duties, disabilities, and other barriers. Oftentimes, students in these populations have also been disproportionately affected by the pandemic. The American College Health Association names Black, Latinx, Asian American, first-generation low-income, LGBTQ+, Native American, international and unauthorized students, and students with disabilities as those who have been disproportionately affected by the pandemic.[2] Some students fall into more than one of these categories.

The authors provide practical advice for those working in academic libraries to address unique challenges and provide inspiring ideas in response to the rising numbers of at-risk students in colleges and universities, and the impact of the COVID-19 pandemic on the students it has affected the most. This book represents a wide variety of topics in librarianship, including open textbooks, internships, programming, and teaching, with practical ideas that can be applied as libraries move forward.

As hubs of learning that serve the entire population of students, academic libraries must be prepared to support a variety of students, from first-year, to parenting students, first-generation students, and students facing financial strain and other barriers.

Part I: Support in Rapidly Changing Learning Environments

Academic librarians creatively supported and engaged with students during the sudden and large-scale shift to online learning caused by the pandemic. Going forward, successful libraries will need to transform their business models to respond to permanently expanded online teaching, provide related professional development for library staff, shift collection expenditures to increase their online collections, and prioritize work that supports students who are learning remotely. Increased embedded librarianship, virtual research help, and new policies for interlibrary loan and special collections are only a few of the innovations the pandemic prompted in libraries that will create lasting positive changes for students, especially as student bodies become more diverse and nontraditional.

As greater numbers of students juggle family and work commitments in addition to school, colleges and universities are increasingly adapting their courses to be more flexible by providing asynchronous and synchronous online courses, self-paced classes, and evening classes. Libraries too, are shifting their support mechanisms in order to be flexible for students who have a multitude of commitments.

Part 1 of this book has chapters describing best practices for supporting students as remote learners and in a continually evolving landscape. It contains chapters on how libraries are adapting to changes in colleges' educational structures, student bodies, course content, and financial resources. The chapters touch upon policies and partnerships, new models for providing research assistance, hiring considerations for libraries (i.e., night librarians, first-year librarians), working in asynchronous and synchronous online environments, creating self-paced library instruction modules and videos, methods of book delivery, and more.

- Garczynski created a makerspace to develop data skills to prepare students for a rapidly growing job market demanding those abilities.
- Pickard and Desilets have taken significant steps to integrate information literacy instruction into STEM courses at Portland State University, where 33 percent of STEM majors are first-generation students.
- VanDyne and Koszalka suggest ways that libraries can address inequities among rural community college students, especially during crises like the pandemic.
- Simms, Haskins, and McDonald foster connections with students by practicing instruction based on warmth and empathy.
- Fielder-Giscombe and Toth developed new models of reference services to support students at their predominately Black institution during the pandemic.
- Matthews and Gaspar partnered with teaching faculty to reframe existing services for greater accessibility during and after the pandemic.

Part II: Programming That Fosters Inclusion

Library programming and outreach events are learning opportunities and ways to encourage students' social integration into college life, a key factor in the retention of undergraduates. Programming engages students with the library and its resources and provides effective ways to reach students in need and to promote equity and inclusion. Libraries can support students through programming for specific demographics, well-being, and mentoring. For example:

- Clement implemented library services at a dorm for first-generation students at her university.
- Kletscher and Tirrell launched a virtual and interactive art exhibit and program fostering cultural competencies and inclusivity.
- Tariana Smith discusses foundational tools for inclusive programming.
- Coleman, Pankl, and Lo advocate for library programming that focuses on supporting the physical and mental well-being of students.
- Reale empowers student employees through impactful mentoring.

Part III: Libraries Providing Financial Support

A central mission of a library is to remove the financial and physical barriers to resources, making them freely accessible and facilitating learning and research. Students facing financial barriers to buying textbooks, laptops, and other resources are more at risk of dropping out of college, and libraries are inventing ways to remove these barriers. Libraries are building on this mission as new technology and resources become available, offering OER and OA materials for courses, free Wi-Fi, laptop checkouts, and safe spaces to study and spend time. Moreover, libraries can provide additional financial support to students by employing them. Part 3 includes innovative ways that libraries are easing the financial burden of college by addressing technology inequities, launching e-textbook initiatives, and offering paid internships. For example:

- Felicia Smith partnered with a local prep school to provide paid library internships to low-income students from underrepresented minority groups.
- Wilkinson and her colleagues expanded an already robust open-textbook program in response to the pandemic, reducing textbook costs for more students.

- Wilson's library bridged a digital divide during the pandemic by providing free hotspots and a personal librarian to students from rural Appalachia.
- Dew, Mitchell, and Mythen partnered with a public library to provide and distribute laptops to low-income students impacted by the pandemic.
- Stoothoff examines different approaches to providing paid library work to first-generation and low-income students.

Through successful case studies and examples from a variety of academic libraries, readers will be able to identify ideas and resources that have worked in other libraries that best fit their own situations in order to flourish after the pandemic. They will learn about news ways to engage with those students who need the most support, and will have a current resource on how libraries are responding to changes brought about by the pandemic, movements of racial reckoning, and their ripple effects on campuses' curriculums, budgets, and student demographics.

NOTES

1. Madeline St. Amour, "As Times and Students Change, Can Faculty Change, Too?" *Inside Higher Ed*, April 2, 2020, www.insidehighered.com/news/2020/04/03/faculty-face-uphill-battle-adapting-needs-todays-students.
2. "ACHA Guidelines: Supporting Vulnerable Campus Populations during the COVID-19 Pandemic," American College Health Association, August 2020, www.acha.org/documents/resources/guidelines/ACHA_Supporting_Vulnerable_Populations_During_the_COVID-19_Pandemic_August2020.pdf.

Part I

Support in Rapidly Changing Learning Environments

JOYCE GARCZYNSKI

Taking a Byte Out of the Data Divide

How an Academic Library Made Data Skills More Accessible by Creating a Makerspace

Data-related jobs are among some of the fastest growing in the United States. Glassdoor has rated data scientist as a best job in America for three of the last five years.[1] Data skills are more in demand across a number of professions, from marketing to journalism, to geography, to the hard sciences. To prepare for these careers, students must learn data literacy skills, such as how to find, interpret, and represent data. They also need to have ready access to the technology to be able to put those skills into practice.

Unfortunately, many college and university students do not have personal access to this technology. In 2018, about 20 percent of college students surveyed responded that they had difficulty maintaining access to digital technology, with students of color disproportionately impacted.[2] The COVID-19 pandemic exacerbated this divide. In summer 2020, 62 percent of Latinx college students and 50 percent of Black college students reported that having access to reliable, high-speed internet was problematic.[3]

Academic libraries have the ability to mitigate this divide by providing access to the technology tools and literacy skills that students need to launch successful data careers. In large part, it has been the research-intensive, or R1, university libraries that have created such data programs. These elite institutions and their libraries, however, are not accessible to many Black and Latinx college students. A report from the Education Trust found that "the overwhelming majority of the nation's most selective public colleges are still inaccessible for Black and Latino undergraduates."[4] So how can smaller, non-research-intensive academic libraries provide these vital services and resources to the vulnerable students who need them the most?

This chapter provides a case study on how one academic library, Towson University's Albert S. Cook Library, a single library at a public doctoral and professional university with an expanding and racially diverse student population,[5] successfully created a data studio in order to expand access to data skills on its campus. The case study will address how the library staff assessed the need for this makerspace, determined the resources and services to be included in the space, obtained financial and technological resources to support the space, and promoted the space to campus constituencies. This case study also discusses how the data studio has impacted campus discussions about data skills and how this space will move forward after the COVID-19 pandemic.

Starting with an Idea

In 2018, makerspaces were a trending topic on many university campuses. It was no different at Towson University (in Towson, Maryland), and many of its departments sought to create areas where students have access to specialized equipment to build and create. The administration of the Albert S. Cook Library wanted the library to have a makerspace of its own, and made a compelling case for placing a makerspace in there. The library is centrally located on campus, and prior to the pandemic, was open 110 hours per week, with more than 20,000 people visiting the library each week, making it one of the most popular spaces on campus.

However, the library needed to address three substantial challenges before opening a makerspace:

1. How could the library create a makerspace that would benefit the campus? The space would need to align with the university's strategic goals yet be different from the specialized spaces that other departments were creating.
2. How could the library fund a makerspace? Acquiring makerspace technology and then continuing to provide the materials needed

to operate that technology would require an initial investment, followed by ongoing support. For example, a professional-grade 3D printer costs between $4,000 and $10,000 to purchase, and the filament to print costs around $20 per kilogram.[6] Because Towson University has a large population of more than 20,000 students, introducing and maintaining some of the typical maker technology would require spending hundreds of thousands of dollars for start-up and ongoing costs.
3. How could the library create interest in the makerspace after it opens? While too much use would not be financially sustainable, too little use would make it difficult to justify continued funding as technology upgrades are needed. What campus partners would be best to help get a library makerspace started?

Although addressing these challenges was an ambitious undertaking, I developed a possible solution. After observing that an increasing number of courses from across the university included data analysis, data visualization, and mapping-related assignments, and that more students were struggling to access the software needed to complete these assignments, I had an idea for creating a makerspace that would focus on data. In order to transform this idea into a reality, I would need to refine the concept, obtain funding, and build partnerships to promote the space.

Refining the Concept

I first shared the idea for a data-focused makerspace in the library with my supervisor, the dean of the University Libraries. I prepared talking points about how data skills aligned with the university's strategic goal of preparing graduates for twenty-first-century careers and how providing data literacy education fit within the library's mission. The dean, however, wanted to talk more about practicalities and asked about the space's size, hardware, software, and service models. She tasked me with further developing the concept and creating a one-sheet prospectus describing the proposed space.

In order to respond to the dean's request for additional information, I researched academic library makerspaces and talked with the staff at two other libraries that had data-related makerspaces. During these interviews, I asked the following questions:

1. How did your data makerspace get started?
2. Did you have any pushback when opening your space? If so, from whom, and how did you overcome that pushback?
3. How is your data makerspace configured?
4. Who uses your makerspace the most? Why do you think that is?
5. How is your makerspace promoted to potential users?
6. How is your space managed? Do you like the setup you have or do you want to change it?
7. What technology do you have?
8. What technology gets the most use? By whom?
9. What technology do you regret purchasing?
10. What technology do you wish you had?
11. What other wishes do you have for your data makerspace?
12. If you could make one change today in your data makerspace, what would it be?

Even though the interviewed libraries were part of universities with higher research profiles than Towson, these in-depth interviews proved to be invaluable. Based on the other libraries' responses, I proposed a data makerspace on the main floor of the library. It would start off small, with four individual workstations and one group workstation, but it would contain flexible furniture and movable walls to enable the space to grow with increased demand. The technology would be limited to high-powered PCs with data analysis, data visualization, and mapping software. Expensive equipment such as a 3D printer would not be included, because the libraries we interviewed said theirs got little use.

I drafted a one-page prospectus for the space, which discussed the growth in data science careers; how a data makerspace would connect with both the university's and the library's strategic goals for a more diverse and inclusive campus; why the library was the best place for this data makerspace; and what technology the space would contain. The dean presented the prospectus to campus leadership, including the provost, in order to obtain his support for the concept. The dean and I also built a coalition of supportive departments, such as the Department of Geography and Environmental Planning and the Faculty Academic Center of Excellence at Towson (FACET). After each meeting, I sent the prospectus to everyone in the meeting to serve as a reminder and ensure that supporters could speak effectively about the project.

The dean also obtained the library staff's support for a data makerspace by involving them in the project. The location selected for the makerspace was occupied by the library's dwindling print reference collection. The staff and librarians organized a project to further remove outdated materials from that collection and consolidate the shelves so that the new data makerspace could occupy that area.

Funding the Project

In order to make the data makerspace a reality, the library needed to obtain funding for the space's furniture, high-powered PCs, and software. I worked with the dean of libraries and the head of library information technology to acquire contributions from donors, secure campus funding, and explore free or low-cost options to create the data makerspace.

The most expensive component of creating the data makerspace was the new furniture that would occupy the space. While furniture from other areas of the building could have been cobbled together to furnish the space, it would not have made the space inviting to new users. Because this would be a one-time expense, a grant or a donor's gift was the best course of action to secure funding for the furniture. The dean of libraries and I approached two individual donors who had previously established a fund to support library innovation. We met with the donors over lunch, presented the data makerspace concept to them, and provided them with a folder full of detailed information about the proposed space. It included the prospectus, a preliminary budget, an architectural rendering of the space, and examples of data visualizations that could be created using software that would be in the space. The donors took the folder home with them so they could further explore the concept, and then the dean followed up with a phone call to them three days after the lunch meeting, and the donors agreed to fund the new data makerspace.

In order to fund the hardware and software that would go into the space, I teamed up with the head of library information technology to apply for the use of student technology fees. Towson University has a process whereby campus units that operate student computer labs can apply for these funds that students pay in addition to their tuition. The application to use student technology fees for the library's data makerspace brought the project to the attention of the campus information technology unit, and they had excellent suggestions for what technology would work best in the space. After the request was approved, the campus information technology unit became invested in the data makerspace and agreed to include the space's technology in their annual update cycle for the campus.

Obtaining funding for software proved to be the most challenging part. Towson University has a rigorous process that looks at accessibility and sustainability before purchasing new software, so the team creating the data makerspace decided to limit adding new, paid software to the computers. This meant that the team prioritized adding data analysis, data visualization, and mapping software that the university had already purchased, as well as new open-source software. The team planned to open the data makerspace with a core group of programs that met these criteria and then consider adding additional paid programs later if there was a demand for them.

The funding we were able to obtain shaped the makerspace that we were able to create. The funding from individual donors enabled us to purchase distinctive furniture to make the space appealing. The support from Towson University allowed us to purchase the high-powered technology that is fundamental to making data skills more accessible to vulnerable populations. In addition, the lack of funding for software meant that we were limited in terms of what we could initially include in the space. Ultimately, both internal and external funding proved vital in creating a significant data makerspace at Towson University.

Creating Interest

A library data makerspace would only be able to mitigate the digital divide if students knew about the space and had access to its technology. As a result, marketing and promoting the space was critical to its success. I focused these efforts in three key areas: branding, partnerships, and outreach.

In 2019 Towson University launched a new brand, including a new logo and a shift in messaging. Towson now refers to itself as TU, and many of the marketing materials include words with TU in the middle, such as "momentum." I incorporated this new university brand into the library makerspace, hoping to make it easier for the university to publicize the space when it opened. I named the space the Data Studio, which includes a TU in the middle, and incorporated the new logo into the signage for the space.

The official opening of the Cook Library's Data Studio took place on February 26, 2020. It included a ribbon-cutting and an open house with more than fifty supporters, partners, and donors in attendance (see figure 1.1). The provost gave a speech and referred to the space as "transformative" for the campus. The university's marketing unit took pictures of the event and produced a story that was shared with newsrooms across the region. I even had conversations with two or three faculty members in attendance about support for their course assignments that semester. Three weeks later, the university made the decision to suspend all in-person instruction on campus due to the COVID-19 pandemic, and the library remained closed for almost six months.

FIGURE 1.1
Data Studio's ribbon-cutting ceremony

The closure of the library and the brand-new Data Studio meant that I needed to shift our promotional efforts to focus on established partnerships. Many of the faculty members who attended the ribbon-cutting and had voiced interest in incorporating the Data Studio into their courses decided to remove the data-related assignments from their syllabi because their students were now struggling with access to the necessary technology. One faculty member in the Business Analytics and Technology Management Department, however, decided to move forward with launching a campus-wide data analysis and visualization competition. With the hope of increasing interest in data analysis at Towson, the faculty member had begun planning the competition before the ribbon-cutting and did not want to lose momentum. Accordingly, in the 2020 fall semester, twelve teams of students from across the campus competed for a $2,500 first prize for producing the best analysis and visualization of data provided by the competition's sponsor, the university's Office of Alumni Relations. I worked with the faculty member to establish the competition and find funding for the prizes. I also served as a mentor for the students participating in the competition and as a judge. The students who participated in the data competition were surprised to learn about the existence of the Data Studio, and hoped that the space would get more use when students fully returned to campus after the COVID-19 pandemic.

Looking to the Future

Towson University's Albert S. Cook Library sought to create a data makerspace in order to provide every TU student with access to the technology they need to gain these in-demand skills. From developing the concept to cutting the ribbon and opening the space, the process to build the Cook Library's Data Studio took two years. During this time, library staff forged a number of partnerships with faculty and administrators in order to connect students with the technology they needed to complete their data-related assignments. While the COVID-19 pandemic forced the project to change course, the data analysis and visualization competition demonstrated a real need for and interest in the acquisition of data skills across campus, and this will surely gain more momentum as life returns to normal. The COVID-19 pandemic has demonstrated the impact that unequal access to technology can have on students' ability to learn. This divide will not disappear with the end of the pandemic, and Towson University's data makerspace has the potential to mitigate this divide.

The key to ensuring the Data Studio's success moving forward will be the resumption of outreach and partnerships once students and courses return to campus for in-person learning. The campus-wide data analysis and data visualization competition will likely continue, but I believe that the continued integration of data skills into course assignments will ensure the space's long-term success. Having this technology in the library will encourage faculty members to include data skills in their syllabi because they know that every student will have equal access to the technology needed to be successful. Thus, I am committed to continued outreach so that all Towson University students' data skills can truly be transformed.

NOTES

1. "50 Best Jobs in America for 2021," Glassdoor, 2021, www.glassdoor.com/List/Best-Jobs-in-America-LST_KQ0,20.htm.
2. Amy L. Gonzales, Jessica McCrory Calarco, and Teresa Lynch, "Technology Problems and Student Achievement Gaps: A Validation and Extension of the Technology Maintenance Construct," *Communication Research* 47, no. 5 (2020): 750, https://doi.org/10.1177/0093650218796366.
3. "New America Higher Ed Survey," Global Strategy Group, 2020, http://thirdway.imgix.net/New-America-and-Third-Way-Higher-Ed-Student-Polling-Data.pdf.
4. "'Segregation Forever?' The Continued Underrepresentation of Black and Latino Undergraduates at the Nation's 101 Most Selective Public Colleges and Universities," Education Trust, 2020, https://edtrust.org/wp-content/uploads/2014/09/Segregation-Forever-The-Continued-Underrepresentation-of-Black-and-Latino-Undergraduates-at-the-Nations-101-Most-Selective-Public-Colleges-and-Universities-July-21-2020.pdf.
5. Kyle Hobstetter, "TU Ranked as One of the Country's Most Diverse Campuses," Towson University, 2019, www.towson.edu/news/2019/usnwr-diversecampus.html.
6. "How Much Does a 3D Printer Cost To Buy and Maintain in 2021?" 3D Sourced, 2021, www.3dsourced.com/3d-printers/how-much-does-a-3d-printer-cost-price.

ELIZABETH PICKARD AND MICHELLE R. DESILETS

Small Victories in STEM Librarianship

Taking on the Big Problem of Missing Information Literacy Instruction in Science Curricula and the Case of First-Generation Students

In 2013, the National Center for Education Statistics reported a pattern of first-generation college students trailing their continuing-generation peers in persistence in STEM fields.[1] Recognizing this trend, a 2019 *Inside Higher Ed* article proposed that targeted, integrated support contributes to first-generation STEM students' academic persistence.[2] Information literacy instruction (ILI) is widely accepted as an important form of academic support for students, and while a 2017 *Library Journal* survey shows that ILI is a particularly important form of support for many first-generation college students, research also indicates a lack of this type of instruction in STEM curricula.[3]

The authors' own experiences as science librarians at Portland State University (PSU) confirmed that they were not working with STEM students nearly as often as with students in other disciplines, which was especially troubling given PSU's large number of first-generation students. From 2012 to 2019, an average of 36 percent of incoming PSU freshmen identified as first-generation students, and 33 percent of PSU STEM majors were first-generation students.[4] Since traditional outreach was not working to get more ILI into PSU's STEM courses, the authors had to think creatively about other avenues for outreach to STEM faculty. This chapter reports on a case study in which the authors identified outreach opportunities in a university-level initiative to take small but significant steps toward integrating ILI into STEM courses. The study also unearthed the effects of rapid change, such as faculty turnover and the pandemic-related move to remote learning, on the ILI that the librarians were able to implement.

Literature Review

Numerous studies have examined the dearth of underrepresented groups, including first-generation students, in college STEM majors. For example, a six-year longitudinal study of first-time college students found that first-generation students trail their continuing-generation peers in both persistence and degree attainment.[5] The question then arises whether a similar pattern emerges for first-generation students in STEM fields. In fact, research suggests that first-generation college students are often members of multiple underrepresented or vulnerable groups—such as women, older students, low-income, or underrepresented racial and ethnic groups[6]—and Bettencourt et al. "theorize that first-generation status may represent a convenient shorthand for a form of cumulative disadvantage . . . [that] may be uniquely felt by students on STEM pathways."[7] For example, first-generation students appear to be less likely to complete a STEM degree than their continuing-generation peers[8] and sometimes experience lower self-efficacy.[9] The literature has shown a correlation between feelings of self-efficacy, belonging, and the academic achievement and persistence of college students.[10] Shaw and Barbuti's study showed this correlation among STEM students as well; they found that "STEM switchers [that is, students who did not continue to pursue a STEM major] had lower science self-efficacy ratings than did persisters."[11]

While studies show that targeted, integrated support can help first-generation STEM students develop academic self-efficacy and a sense of belonging, very few have looked at information literacy instruction as a source of such support, even though it is widely accepted as an effective means of teaching the research skills that students need to successfully complete their coursework. According to *Inside Higher Ed*, "first-gen, low-income and underrepresented minority students absolutely need support from faculty members in STEM and other academic leaders who can . . . help them address any gaps in educational preparation."[12] Research has generally suggested that academic support is key to first-generation STEM students' persistence[13] and has proposed practices that increase self-efficacy and a sense of belonging as the most beneficial ones in this regard.[14] Other studies have examined specific forms of support, such as intensive writing workshops, workshops that focus on the evaluation of primary literature,[15] and mentoring,[16] but very few studies have looked specifically at ILI as a source of academic support in terms of fostering self-efficacy and a sense of belonging in students. In one such study, Phillips and Zwicky indeed found that ILI increases engineering students' self-efficacy with respect to patent-searching.[17]

This finding is consistent with the authors' thinking that ILI provides exactly the kind of targeted support that bolsters both students' self-efficacy and sense of belonging. In keeping with Albert Bandura's seminal definition of self-efficacy, ILI offers a student "the conviction that one can successfully execute the behavior required to produce the outcomes" or the conviction that one has the "capabilities to produce desired effects."[18] In teaching students information literacy skills and research as an iterative process, ILI formally shows students the skills they need to succeed at their coursework[19] and later as employees in the field.[20] The resulting grades, feedback from instructors, and an improved ability to find more and better sources reinforce the fact that students do, indeed, have the "capabilities to produce desired effects." Bandura explains that this "learning from response consequences" leads students to develop "efficacy expectations [that] determine how much effort [they] will expend and how long they will persist in the face of obstacles and aversive experiences."[21]

In his influential work, Vincent Tinto builds on Bandura's ideas, explaining that "students have to want to persist . . . even when faced with the challenges they sometimes encounter."[22] Tinto connects self-efficacy to belonging, and says: "Students' belief in their ability to succeed in college . . . is not just a reflection of a student's perception of their place in the social environment. It also mirrors their perception of their academic belonging . . . for students who find the demands of the institution excessively challenging."[23] Following Bandura and Tinto's collective logic, because ILI directly supports students' self-efficacy in their coursework, it can facilitate their sense of belonging in academia as well. Furthermore, ILI can help students develop an expectation of efficacy that can bolster them through academic challenges and thus increase the likelihood of their persistence through college.

In fact, since 2006, the ACRL's Information Literacy Standards for Science and Engineering/Technology have specifically called for STEM curricula to include teaching students to identify and evaluate a variety of potential sources of information,[24] and research has correlated those standards with the National Research Council's call for information skills in scientists.[25] Studies have also shown that ILI can have a significant effect on the information literacy of first-generation students compared to first-generation students who do not receive such instruction.[26]

However, an examination of the literature also reveals that despite a demonstrated need for information literacy instruction, it is lacking in most STEM courses. STEM curricula often focus on creating and working with data rather than developing literature reviews.[27] When students are assigned to write a literature review, studies show that STEM majors in disciplines such as physical geography often rely on their instructors to both disseminate sources and point to specific experts in the field.[28] This reliance on the instructor raises questions about whether STEM students are able to find and evaluate sources on their own.

While some faculty members assume that students enter college already possessing these skills,[29] Perry's study of STEM faculty revealed that "faculty overwhelmingly expressed concerns with the critical thinking skills of students and their inability to evaluate the sources that they are reading."[30] Faculty further indicated that students often overestimate their own information literacy skills, underestimate the amount of time that research takes—that is, they fail to view research as an iterative process—and do not seem able to distinguish between types of information. Clearly, the scarcity of ILI in STEM curricula is a wide-reaching problem that has serious implications for students.

The implications of this ILI-scarcity may be particularly serious for first-generation students whose persistence depends on such support. This chapter reports on outreach opportunities that two PSU science librarians identified during their work on a university-level initiative, how they leveraged these incidental opportunities to increase ILI in STEM courses, and how faculty turnover and the sudden move to remote learning affected the ILI they had implemented.

Background and Methodology

At Portland State University, some departments prefer their subject librarian to restrict contact to an appointed department member, while others welcome the librarian's contact with all department faculty. In the examples discussed in this chapter, two librarians (the authors) serve as liaisons to multiple STEM departments: Biology, Environmental Science and Management (ESM), Geography, Geology, and Systems Science. The authors began their tenures as science librarians at PSU in 2014 and 2019, respectively. Their initial ILI outreach efforts consisted of e-mail messages introducing themselves, as well as a quarterly library newsletter, both following the communication preferences set by the departments. However, these efforts were not successful in integrating more ILI into STEM courses. Starting in 2016, the authors identified new outreach opportunities incidental to a university-level initiative that resulted in the inclusion of ILI in several additional STEM courses.

Case Findings

The authors had taught very few ILI sessions for STEM classes in the years leading up to 2016, around which time a university-level initiative created opportunities for new kinds of outreach. PSU's Flexible Degree initiative is a program through which the university's Office of Academic Innovation (OAI) offers financial, project management, and instructional design support to departments which are developing new online degree programs. The OAI invited subject librarians to participate in its Flexible Degree planning meetings. Through this initiative, the librarians identified and attempted to leverage incidental outreach opportunities, which led to small but significant increases in the number of ILI sessions librarians provided for their STEM departments.

Between 2012 and 2016, PSU librarians taught ILI sessions for a total of only three ESM classes, four geography classes, and one biology class (see table 2.1). Librarians taught no sessions for ESM in the 2012–13 academic year and then only one session per year for the next three years. During that four-year span, librarians taught one session per year for geography, one class, total, for biology, and none for geology or systems science.

TABLE 2.1
Total number of undergraduate ILI sessions before and after new outreach

Department	Before 2012/13 to 2015/16	After 2016/17 to 2019/20
Biology	1	7
ESM	3	14
Geography	4	9
Geology	0	0
Systems Science	0	0
TOTAL	8	30

The departments of ESM and Geography were part of the first round of "flexible degrees," and at the initial OAI meetings, the librarian met five ESM and four geography faculty members she had never met before. During these meetings, the librarian was allotted time for a presentation at which she encouraged teaching faculty to include an ILI session in the new courses. She pointed to PSU-specific parameters that underscore the need for ILI at the university, namely that PSU has no writing or research admissions requirements and that the PSU undergraduate population includes a large percentage of students who may come to academic research with a cumulative disadvantage. The librarian was also able to point to her own research, which shows that scaffolding research skills into course curricula—even in small ways, such as providing students an article citation instead of a PDF for required readings—can accomplish some level of ILI integration and that course-related ILI can actually reduce the instructor's workload.[31]

Within the year, three ESM faculty members from these meetings scheduled ILI sessions for their face-to-face classes. Two others began working with the librarian to incorporate library exercises and PSU Library video tutorials into their asynchronous online courses and to scaffold research skills across their curricula. In the beginning, neither of these instructors was aware of the library's research guides (LibGuides). The faculty reported that these discussions with the librarian facilitated shifts in their pedagogical approaches to teaching research and that they now regularly refer students to the ESM subject guide and assign exercises that require students to use the guide. These relationships have continued even five years later, through PSU's rapid shift to remote learning as a result of the pandemic. These same ESM faculty sought the librarian's input on ways to integrate ILI into the courses which they suddenly had to move online.

In the terms immediately following the Flexible Degree meetings, three geography faculty members also requested ILI sessions for their existing courses. The librarians' work with flexible degrees indirectly affected the number of ILI sessions taught for biology courses as well, when an ESM faculty member who had taken part in the Flexible Degree initiative began to teach biology courses with ILI included.

The cumulative results of this incidental outreach were an increase from three to fourteen ILI sessions in ESM classes, from four to nine sessions in geography classes, and from one to seven sessions in biology classes (see table 2.1). Furthermore, the librarians went from teaching sessions for only one faculty member per department to working with three in geography, four in ESM, and two in biology, that is, working with six additional faculty members. In terms of the effects on students, one ESM faculty member conducted an end-of-term survey of students who had attended an ILI session with the librarian and reported: "34 out of 36 students said that they are now better able to investigate and evaluate questions of science using the library resources! For those students [for whom] this was new (not those two who didn't learn new things), they were very excited about learning how to do this, and actually really use their library. . . . Several said they use the library and databases all of the time now." In contrast, the departments of Geology and Systems Science, for which there have not yet been flexible degree initiatives, have seen no increase in ILI sessions taught for undergraduate classes (table 2.1).

Discussion

Ultimately, the librarians' work with flexible degrees more than tripled the number of ILI sessions across the STEM subjects this chapter discusses, increasing the total from eight sessions to thirty (table 2.1). Thus, the small outreach victories in each department led to an overall significant impact which supported many more STEM students, including the nearly one-third who identified as first-generation college students. This work also strengthened relationships between the librarians and the STEM departments by increasing the number of faculty members in each department for whom the librarians taught ILI sessions. The strengthened relationships served as a kind of buffer during the pandemic-related rapid shift to remote learning and during the more predictable changes caused by faculty turnover. Even when an ESM faculty member left, ESM students continued to receive ILI in other ESM courses. During the pandemic-related move to remote learning, it was those same ESM faculty members who requested the only ILI sessions.

Why This Outreach Seemed to Work

While librarians at other institutions will not encounter exactly the same outreach opportunities, aspects of this initiative are transferable to other contexts. In other words, librarians can be prepared to take advantage of incidental opportunities that:

Target a specific course—The initiative pertained to a specific course or set of courses, which contextualized the librarians' outreach as immediately relevant compared to unsolicited e-mail messages.

Occur at the point of curriculum development—The outreach occurred at the same time that instructors were developing the course curriculum, that is, at the point of need.

Position the librarian as part of a team of experts—The initiative emphasized the fact that librarians have expertise, specifically expertise that is not only relevant but necessary to course curricula.

Designate time
- As part of a larger initiative, the outreach did not require teaching faculty to expend extra time or effort in order to meet with the librarian.
- Positioning the librarian as part of a team implicitly created the expectation that everyone on the team, including the librarian,

would have input. This allowed for a different kind of outreach conversation:
- Because this outreach was not a "cold call," the teaching faculty expected the librarian's input rather than potentially seeing it as another "to do" e-mail response.
- Rather than broadly listing their services, the librarians had time to delve into nuances of their expertise. They could discuss their librarian-specific lenses on PSU statistics and the relevant literature and could assume that the teaching faculty were inclined to listen.

What This Case Revealed about Targeted Services to Vulnerable Students under Rapid Change

The rapid move to remote learning during the pandemic resulted in most information literacy instruction being cut from courses in the STEM departments discussed in this chapter. From 2019 to 2021, the number of ILI sessions went from multiple ones per year in biology, ESM, and geography to one session in biology, one in geography, and two in ESM. This sudden decrease demonstrates that such targeted support can be vulnerable under circumstances of rapid change, and this reduction in targeted services leaves vulnerable students—who might be at even more risk in such uncertain times—even more vulnerable.

The rapid shift also points to the importance of establishing relationships with teaching faculty, as evidenced by the fact that three of the four ILI sessions the librarians taught in 2019–21 were for faculty members they met during the planning for the Flexible Degrees Initiative. It is worth noting that the ILI already integrated into curricula, for example, the ESM syllabi giving citations rather than PDFs for required readings, may have endured as faculty transitioned their courses to a remote learning environment.

Conclusion and Future Research

The findings from this case study can help librarians both seek out and create opportunities for meaningful outreach, outreach that can lead to the incorporation of much-needed ILI in STEM college course curricula. The findings also show how even small steps can grow important relationships that serve to buffer the targeted services, such as ILI, which support vulnerable student populations during periods of rapid change.

The authors approached the study with the idea that increasing information literacy instruction would inherently (and strategically) support first-generation students by increasing the self-efficacy and sense of belonging of all students. However, future research might extend these findings to look at nuances of ILI's effects on first-generation STEM students' self-efficacy and sense of belonging, their research practices, their persistence in college, and their persistence in STEM. Future research might also examine the implications of college ILI (or the lack of it) on research conducted later in professional and postgraduate academic STEM settings. Thus, findings from this and future studies can inform librarians' practice so that they are prepared to seize incidental but important opportunities for outreach, which when successful, can result in small successes that have significant impact.

NOTES

1. Xianglei Chen, "STEM Attrition: College Students' Paths into and out of STEM Fields," Statistical Analysis Report, NCES 2014-001, National Center for Education Statistics, Institute of Education Sciences, U.S. Department of Education, 2013, https://files.eric.ed.gov/fulltext/ED544470.pdf.
2. Adrianna Kezar and Elizabeth Holcombe, "An Overlooked Solution for Diversifying STEM," *Insider Higher Ed*, January 14, 2019, www.insidehighered.com/views/2019/01/14/recommendations-making-stem-education-more-diverse-opinion.
3. *Library Journal*, "First-Year Experience Survey: Information Literacy in Higher Education," March 2017, https://s3.amazonaws.com/WebVault/research/LJ_FirstYearExperienceSurvey_Mar2017.pdf.
4. "Portland State University First-Generation Student Statistics: 2012–2019," Portland State University, Office of Institutional Research and Planning, 2021.
5. Emily Forrest Cataldi, Emily Forrest, Christopher T. Bennett, and Xianglei Chen, "First-Generation Students: College Access, Persistence, and Postbachelor's Outcomes," NCES 2018-421, Statistics in Brief, National Center for Education Statistics, Institute of Education Sciences, U.S. Department of Education, 2018, https://files.eric.ed.gov/fulltext/ED580935.pdf.

6. Sandra L. Dika and Mark M. D'Amico, "Early Experiences and Integration in the Persistence of First-Generation College Students in STEM and Non-STEM Majors," *Journal of Research in Science Teaching* 53, no. 3 (2016): 368–83, https://doi.org/10.1002/tea.21301.
7. Genia M. Bettencourt, Catherine A. Manly, Ezekiel Kimball, and Ryan S. Wells, "STEM Degree Completion and First-Generation College Students: A Cumulative Disadvantage Approach to the Outcomes Gap," *Review of Higher Education* 43, no. 3 (2020): 753–79, https://doi.org/10.1353/rhe.2020.0006.
8. Bettencourt et al., "STEM Degree Completion," 762–63; Emily J. Shaw and Sandra Barbuti, "Patterns of Persistence in Intended College Major with a Focus on STEM Majors," *NACADA Journal* 30, no. 2 (2010): 19–34, https://doi.org/10.12930/0271-9517-30.2.19.
9. Lucila Ramos-Sánchez and Laura Nichols, "Self-Efficacy of First-Generation and Non-First-Generation College Students: The Relationship with Academic Performance and College Adjustment," *Journal of College Counseling* 10, no. 1 (2007): 6–18, https://doi.org/10.1002/j.2161-1882.2007.tb00002.x; Stephanie Cornelia Aymans and Simone Kauffeld, "To Leave or Not to Leave? Critical Factors for University Dropout among First-Generation Students," *Zeitschrift für Hochschulentwicklung*, December 2015, https://doi.org/10.3217/zfhe-10-04/02.
10. Paul A. Gore, "Academic Self-Efficacy as a Predictor of College Outcomes: Two Incremental Validity Studies," *Journal of Career Assessment* 14, no. 1 (2006): 92–115, https://doi.org/10.1177/1069072705281367; Karen D. Multon, Steven D. Brown, and Robert W. Lent, "Relation of Self-Efficacy Beliefs to Academic Outcomes: A Meta-Analytic Investigation," *Journal of Counseling Psychology* 38, no. 1 (1991): 30–38, http://dx.doi.org.proxy.lib.pdx.edu/10.1037/0022-0167.38.1.30; Michelle Richardson, Charles Abraham, and Rod Bond, "Psychological Correlates of University Students' Academic Performance: A Systematic Review and Meta-Analysis," *Psychological Bulletin* 138, no. 2 (2012): 353–87, http://dx.doi.org.proxy.lib.pdx.edu/10.1037/a0026838; Steven B. Robbins, Kristy Lauver, Huy Le, Daniel Davis, Ronelle Langley, and Aaron Carlstrom, "Do Psychosocial and Study Skill Factors Predict College Outcomes? A Meta-Analysis," *Psychological Bulletin* 130, no. 2 (2004): 261–88, http://dx.doi.org.proxy.lib.pdx.edu/10.1037/0033-2909.130.2.261.
11. Shaw and Barbuti, "Patterns of Persistence," 26.
12. Kezar and Holcombe, "An Overlooked Solution," para. 9.
13. Dika and D'Amico, "Early Experiences."
14. Byron Hempel, Kasi Kiehlbaugh, and Paul Blowers, "Scalable and Practical Teaching Practices Faculty Can Deploy to Increase Retention: A Faculty Cookbook for Increasing Student Success," *Education for Chemical Engineers* 33 (October 2020): 45–65, https://doi.org/10.1016/j.ece.2020.07.004; Matthew D. Johnson, Amy E. Sprowles, Katlin R. Goldenberg, Steven T. Margell, and Lisa

Castellino, "Effect of a Place-Based Learning Community on Belonging, Persistence, and Equity Gaps for First-Year STEM Students," *Innovative Higher Education* 45, no. 6 (2020): 509–31, https://doi.org/10.1007/s10755-020-09519-5; Emily E. Liptow, Katherine C. Chen, Robin Parent, Jaclyn Duerr, and Dylan Henson, "A Sense of Belonging: Creating a Community for First-Generation, Underrepresented Groups and Minorities through an Engineering Student Success Course," in *Association for Engineering Education – Engineering Library Division Papers* (Atlanta, GA: American Society for Engineering Education-ASEE, 2016), http://dx.doi.org.proxy.lib.pdx.edu/10.18260/p.26439.

15. Carol A. Kozeracki, Michael F. Carey, John Colicelli, and Marc Levis-Fitzgerald, "An Intensive Primary-Literature–Based Teaching Program Directly Benefits Undergraduate Science Majors and Facilitates Their Transition to Doctoral Programs," *CBE—Life Sciences Education* 5, no. 4 (2006): 340–47, https://doi.org/10.1187/cbe.06-02-0144; George M. Malacinski and Brian Winterman, "Engaging and Motivating Undergraduate Science Students in a Writing Workshop Designed to Achieve Information Literacy and Professional Level Competence," *International Journal of Arts & Sciences* 5, no. 6 (2012): 397–414.

16. David MacPhee, Samantha Farro, and Silvia Sara Canetto, "Academic Self-Efficacy and Performance of Underrepresented STEM Majors: Gender, Ethnic, and Social Class Patterns," *Analyses of Social Issues and Public Policy* 13, no. 1 (2013): 347–69, https://doi.org/10.1111/asap.12033.

17. Margaret Phillips and Dave Zwicky, "Information Literacy in Engineering Technology Education: A Case Study," *Journal of Engineering Technology* (Fall 2018), https://docs.lib.purdue.edu/lib_fsdocs/210.

18. Albert Bandura, "Self-Efficacy: Toward a Unifying Theory of Behavioral Change," *Psychological Review* 84, no. 2 (1977): 191–215, http://dx.doi.org.proxy.lib.pdx.edu/10.1037/0033-295X.84.2.191.

19. Aditia Bandyopadhyay, "Measuring the Disparities between Biology Undergraduates' Perceptions and Their Actual Knowledge of Scientific Literature with Clickers," *Journal of Academic Librarianship* 39, no. 2 (2013): 194–201, https://doi.org/10.1016/j.acalib.2012.10.006; Anna Hulseberg and Anna Versluis, "Integrating Information Literacy into an Undergraduate Geography Research Methods Course," *College & Undergraduate Libraries* 24, no. 1 (2017): 14–28, https://doi.org/10.1080/10691316.2017.1251371; Mary B. Kimsey and S. Lynn Cameron, "Teaching and Assessing Information Literacy in a Geography Program," *Journal of Geography* 104, no. 1 (2005): 17–23.

20. Gordon Clark and Martin Higgitt, "Geography and Lifelong Learning: A Report on a Survey of Geography Graduates," *Journal of Geography in Higher Education* 21, no. 2 (1997): 199–213, https://doi.org/10.1080/03098269708725425; Jon Jeffryes and Meghan Lafferty, "Gauging Workplace Readiness: Assessing the Information Needs of Engineering Co-Op Students," *Issues in Science and Technology Librarianship* (Spring 2012), https://doi.org/10.5062/F4X34VDR;

Kimsey and Cameron, "Teaching and Assessing Information Literacy"; Kozeracki, Carey, Colicelli, and Levis-Fitzgerald, "Primary-Literature–Based Teaching"; Malacinski and Winterman, "Engaging and Motivating"; Jenni Simonsen, Laura Sare, and Sarah Bankston, "Creating and Assessing an Information Literacy Component in an Undergraduate Specialized Science Class," *Science & Technology Libraries* 36, no. 2 (2017): 200–218, https://doi.org/ 10.1080/0194262X.2017.1320261.

21. Bandura, "Self-Efficacy," 194.
22. Vincent Tinto, "Through the Eyes of Students," *Journal of College Student Retention: Research, Theory & Practice* 19, no. 3 (2017): 254–69, https://doi.org/10.1177/1521025115621917.
23. Tinto, "Through the Eyes of Students," 261–62.
24. ACRL STS Task Force, "Information Literacy Standards for Science and Engineering/Technology," Association of College & Research Libraries, 2006, www.ala.org/acrl/standards/infolitscitech.
25. Jenni Simonsen, Laura Sare, and Sarah Bankston, "Creating and Assessing an Information Literacy Component in an Undergraduate Specialized Science Class," *Science & Technology Libraries* 36, no. 2 (2017): 200–218, https://doi.org/ 10.1080/0194262X.2017.1320261.
26. Elizabeth Pickard and Firouzeh Logan, "The Research Process and the Library: First-Generation College Seniors vs. Freshmen," *College & Research Libraries* 74, no. 4 (2013): 399–415, https://doi.org/10.5860/crl-348; David A. Tyckoson, "Library Service for the First-Generation College Student," in *Teaching the New Library to Today's Users: Reaching International, Minority, Senior Citizens, Gay/Lesbian, First Generation, At-Risk, Graduate and Returning Students, and Distance Learners*, ed. Trudi E. Jacobson and Helene C. Williams (New York: Neal-Schuman, 2000), 89–105.
27. Heidi Blackburn and Ashlee Dere, "Changing the Scholarly Sources Landscape with Geomorphology Undergraduate Students," *Issues in Science and Technology Librarianship* 19 (2016), https://digitalcommons.unomaha.edu/crisslibfacpub/19; Jeanine M. Scaramozzino, "Integrating STEM Information Competencies into an Undergraduate Curriculum," *Journal of Library Administration* 50, no. 4 (2010): 315–33, https://doi.org/10.1080/01930821003666981.
28. Nicholas Bauch and Christina Sheldon, "Tacit Information Literacies in Beginning College Students: Research Pedagogy in Geography," *Harvard Educational Review* 84, no. 3 (2014): 403–23, 427–28; Ruth Panelli and Richard V. Welch, "Teaching Research through Field Studies: A Cumulative Opportunity for Teaching Methodology to Human Geography Undergraduates," *Journal of Geography in Higher Education* 29, no. 2 (2005): 255–77, https://doi.org/10.1080/03098260500130494.
29. Sharon F. McEuen, "How Fluent with Information Technology Are Our Students?" *Educause Quarterly* 24, no. 4 (2001): 8–17; Leigh Thompson and Lisa

Ann Blankinship, "Teaching Information Literacy Skills to Sophomore-Level Biology Majors," *Journal of Microbiology & Biology Education* 16, no. 1 (2015): 29–33, https://doi.org/10.1128/jmbe.v16i1.818.

30. Heather Brodie Perry, "Information Literacy in the Sciences: Faculty Perception of Undergraduate Student Skill," *College & Research Libraries* 78, no. 7 (2017): 964–77, https://doi.org/10.5860/crl.78.7.964.

31. Elizabeth Pickard and Sarah Sterling, "Information Literacy Instruction in Asynchronous Online Courses: Which Approaches Work Best?" *College & Research Libraries* (forthcoming 2022; preprint available in PDXScholar), https://archives.pdx.edu/ds/psu/35309.

HEATHER VANDYNE AND RACHEL KOSZALKA

Identifying and Addressing the Evolving Accessibility Limitations of Rural Community College Students

For many high school students considering college, it is an exciting time of possibilities: the next step in one's personal chapter and the beginning of an academic career. However, in March 2020, that next step seemed to turn into a stumbling block as COVID-19 turned people's ways of life into a very serious health risk. Some high school students planning spring breaks were blindsided with news that those days in the classroom would be their last for several months. Others felt the void of missed proms, sat through virtual graduation ceremonies, and wondered when or if they would ever be able to finally move into their own dorms.

Students were not the only ones thrown off course. Educators who had planned their courses months in advance had to convert them to online-only format with little or no notice. Administrators had to make hard decisions about public safety; and libraries, which have always been a staple for reliable resources and access at no cost, had to close their doors and find new ways to serve patrons from afar. These changes especially affected rural areas, where the digital gap is more prominent compared to more populated areas with more accessibility and better internet quality. Lockdowns and stay-at-home orders meant that libraries could no longer fill their desired role as a physical community hub.[1]

For many, entering the 2020–2021 academic year turned into a time of uncertainty, hesitation, and overwhelming caution, which can be seen reflected in both student enrollment and financial aid data. According to FAFSA, the number of high school seniors applying for financial aid dropped 21 percent going into the fall 2020 semester, with 200,000 fewer first-time students enrolling in community colleges.[2] For those students who did enroll, the stress of the pandemic has affected their academic lives and performance, causing concern among those in instructional and academic support roles.

In the course of one year, librarians and educators performed multiple pivots that demanded innovation and resilience in both students and instructors. To get a sense of how such rapid changes affected students and educators, the authors sent a survey, created through Google Forms, to librarians at two-year community colleges, asking about student interest, participation, and the performance of current students compared to previous years. The survey was a collaborative effort between Allen Community College and Neosho County Community College, with the survey limited to the southeast Kansas area. The survey was intended to highlight the needs and obstacles facing rural community colleges, which typically have fewer resources and less funding than four-year institutions or colleges in more densely populated areas. We received nineteen responses from library staff and instructors from community colleges in Chanute, Coffeyville, Independence, Iola, and Parsons.

This chapter, through the survey results and other examples, aims to suggest ways that libraries can address inequities when serving the needs of rural college students. Faced with fewer options and, because of the pandemic, more restrictions, rural college librarians face more challenges than ever to serve both students and instructors and offer the best in academic success. And during unprecedented circumstances like the COVID-19 pandemic, when little time was given to prepare for a fully online shift, innovation was key for librarians to help their users, whether faculty, staff, or students, transition as seamlessly as possible as the world adjusted to the ever-present "new normal."

The Challenges of Rural Community Colleges

Though information is being published continuously about the impact of COVID-19 on everyday life, little has been studied in higher education that is especially specific to two-year colleges in rural areas. The Center for Community College Student Engagement administered a survey in 2020 asking students about their experiences entering college. More than 3,600 students reported challenges with finances, online accessibility, and being unaware of college support services "to help cope with the stress related to the pandemic."[3] The study does not differentiate between rural, urban, or suburban communities, but based on the results, incoming college students would greatly benefit from increased reminders of services offered by their institutions to assist with their academic success and overall physical and mental health.

A survey of student experiences, conducted by *Inside Higher Ed* and *College Pulse*, found that while students' overall feelings about college in 2020 were somewhat mixed; there were multiple aspects of student life, both socially and academically, that were generally missed due to pandemic restrictions. Two-year students who responded marked "libraries and study spaces" as the third most missed aspect of student life.[4] Though the percentage of community college respondents in that survey was less than 15 percent, it gives a detailed view of the perspectives and obstacles faced by college students. Only 10 percent responded that they had not experienced any problems with online learning. A report from the University of Texas at Austin noted that more than 90 percent of students have used computers to do coursework online, but nearly three out of ten claimed to have unreliable internet at home, and some didn't have internet access at all.[5] Of the obstacles mentioned, accessing resources from libraries and academic support were listed among the top struggles in online learning. In addition, libraries were listed by over a third of all respondents as the main online resource they wanted to be able to continue utilizing virtually after the pandemic.

The Kansas Office of Rural Prosperity conducted a listening tour in 2019 to hear the needs of its rural residents, and found that unreliable broadband was a top concern. That discussion continued into 2020, when connectivity became a more critical piece of communities' infrastructure due to the pandemic. Though such concerns had been addressed before the pandemic by state government officials, the increased need for digital access in work, education, and health care now made broadband a priority for largely rural states and areas with higher poverty.[6]

With an ongoing mission to be the "third place" that people frequent after their homes and workplaces, both public and academic librarians were challenged with making connections that usually result from in-house programs, events, and activities.[7] The positive aspects of such a challenge were the opportunities for librarians to try new methods to connect with students in providing academic support. Virtual relationships require imagination, and Tran and Higgins point out that a library's strongest assets to foster and maintain patron relationships are its librarians and library staff.[8]

Research Method and Response

According to Kendrick and Tritt, instructors are typically seen by students as a primary source of academic support.[9] Due to their critical role in student learning and the amount of time they spend with students, our brief survey was extended to include faculty members to add further insight into student behavior and performance. Broadening the survey provided us with 13 additional responses from instructors, for a total of 32 responses. The majority of instructors and librarians had had issues when having to move from in-person to online learning, whereas those already working with online or hybrid class formats felt prepared for the mid-semester shift. Instructors who didn't have experience with the online format or who traditionally conducted only in-person classes experienced more difficulties with the change.

Eleven of the thirteen instructors surveyed stated that communicating with students became an issue due to the shift. In some cases, a few of them even claimed to notice a rise in cheating. Maintaining solid instructor-student relationships became difficult due to the virtual barrier, and this caused students to disengage and in some cases give up entirely. The librarians surveyed also stated that interacting with students was one of the more difficult aspects during the transition to remote learning. When forced into lockdown, many students faced various forms of isolation simultaneously, including physical and virtual, which decreased their persistence in seeking the connectivity and support they were used to.[10]

Keeping students engaged while losing the ease of in-person communication caused a ripple that affected many students' academic success. Nearly two-thirds of survey respondents stated that they saw a difference in student participation. One librarian observed that "some students did better online, but other students did worse." Though some students were prepared and worked continuously to keep learning in the virtual space, most participants reported observing a decrease in student participation even in the group of highly motivated students, because of a lack of focusing strategies. Other students who were not fully equipped to do online work struggled greatly with participation and overall academic performance. It was among this group of students that instructors said they saw an increase in cheating and a drop in student engagement on assignments like discussion questions. Finally, the latter group of students never fully accepted the online move and, in rare cases, chose to drop some of their classes.

More than half of the participants responded yes when asked if they had witnessed changes in behavior among the majority of students. The written responses indicated that the reasons for the students' behavioral changes included their concerns about viral exposure, self-quarantining, and treating isolation as an extended break from studies, along with difficulty balancing their responsibilities at home. Even among students who remained engaged in class, motivation and engagement levels dropped. Some students gave questionable excuses for not attending or participating in coursework. These changes were mainly due to the barriers that were created (although these were unavoidable) by moving completely online. When students were struggling, they could not visit their usual resources at physical locations to ask for help.

Another barrier that lower-income students faced was internet accessibility. Students who rely heavily on library services and the internet provided by colleges lost that resource when everything on campus shut down. They faced frozen Zoom meetings, e-mail messages failing to send, and the possibility of missed live classes or late assignments due to connectivity issues.[11] On the positive side, some colleges surveyed stated that they added resources that were very beneficial during this time. For example, one institution's library allowed computers and tablets to be borrowed by students for longer periods. This shows that accessibility is more than just broadband and software; it also involves hardware and having those tools available for use in one's coursework. Some instructors commended their library professionals for allowing them to access additional digital resources and providing courses on how to use their organization's online class via Blackboard.

In its guidelines, the American College Health Association noted that "students will need additional support to optimize their learning environment and protect their health and safety to achieve their academic goals."[12] A mixture of responses in the survey related to meeting this challenge. The librarians surveyed launched new online services such as virtual reference, and others purchased hardware such as cameras and headphones to assist with participation in Zoom meetings and online learning. Most of them also expanded or acquired additional databases, which were accessed significantly more during spring 2020 and the 2020–21 academic year. In some cases, instructors found creative ways to meet the demands of the pandemic. One instructor exchanged phone numbers with their students, allowing them to submit their coursework by texting it. Other teachers improved their explanation of lessons through more detailed instructions or videos that went over student requirements step by step.

At Independence Community College (in Independence, Kansas), several instructors met one-on-one with students who had no internet access, due to low income, to give out paper assignments. The students were seen individually on a weekly basis and were expected to complete all assignments given to them by the following meeting. This strategy allowed students with connectivity difficulties and restricted access to resources due to campus and library closures to continue to learn, even though they could not attend class every single day.

Though our survey does not break down its student demographics into specifics such as whether a student is in their second year, just entering college, or is a high-school student participating in concurrent credit courses to receive college credit, the instructors' insight gives a general overview of the changes our students faced during the long closures. While over half of instructors claimed that the number of students who ended up with failing grades increased compared to previous academic years, further research is required to determine if the cause was related to difficulties with accessibility or to the absence of student support services.

Moving beyond Uncertain Times

This research has showed that, sadly, many organizations and institutions were not prepared for the COVID-19 pandemic, and we hope that this is the starting point for more emergency preparedness. So how can librarians better respond to a crisis if something like COVID-19 were to happen again? How do librarians provide equitable services to underserved students? What are ways to bridge the growing digital divide?

One suggestion is for librarians to evaluate their digital resources and ease of access. Three library professionals in the survey responded that they felt ready to meet this challenge, because of how much their institution had already invested in digital resources. Even before the pandemic, students across the board preferred to have academic services available to them twenty-four hours a day, and in a world of smart devices, they expect nearly instantaneous responses.[13] Librarians must determine how easy it is to access their collections, and holding focus groups to this end can help inform their decisions and uncover areas for improvement. Students know what access challenges they have, and their input is an excellent resource.

Physical collections should not be neglected. Even in this digital age, physical resources are widely used, and this is especially true among lower-income or disadvantaged students. No one should assume what a student utilizes or has access to. Libraries strive to embrace change and remain relevant in this digital age, and so they have to think about investing in technology now more than ever. Expanding libraries' physical lending services to technologies like cameras, laptops, tablets, projectors, and wireless hotspots could not only increase circulation numbers but provide valuable resources to underserved students—as well as to instructors who live in rural areas and may have accessibility issues of their own in their quest to conduct classes. The question that follows from this idea is: How will better physical resources help students if campuses are locked down again? For that, institutions should consider their delivery methods. The survey respondents stated that they used curbside pickup services, and some even resorted to mailing resources to students.

Lastly, we suggest making an emergency plan. Be prepared for another worst-case scenario so that students don't get left behind. What are the ways that campuses and libraries can remain a resource to students if a pandemic hits again? In hindsight, shutting down everything created a barrier to underserved students that should not happen again. Institutions should consider partnering with public libraries and government or community organizations with similar goals in youth and education and then pool their resources in order to provide more efficient and effective resources to everyone.

Conclusion

While academic libraries were unprepared to enter an era of infectious disease like no other experienced in living memory, these unprecedented times have revealed how underserved students were impacted and could easily fall behind in such an emergency. The crisis has provided information professionals with an opportunity to evaluate their preparedness and effectiveness in serving the underserved at a time when most everything is unknown. Academic libraries are an essential element in any institution, and while their importance is well known, rural academic libraries need to continuously work to understand and respond to the needs of students and faculty. To satisfy those needs, librarians must be prepared to go beyond collections to technology, hardware, and software.

Though the trauma of the pandemic is one that nobody will forget, the need for accessibility and connection has now taken center stage. Traditional-age students do not know a life before the internet, and now rely on connectivity both inside their academic environments and out. As the delivery medium evolves and student needs change, it is important to be mindful of the challenges that both students and faculty have faced. Librarians should be essential elements in fulfilling the needs of college students and addressing any new issues that arise. Additional research is needed in these areas, but hopefully the ideas discussed here will open a dialogue with those who are working to help students achieve academic success and work towards a quality future.

NOTES

1. Shaun Briley, "Fostering Social Connections and Local Community during a Global Pandemic," in *Pivoting during the Pandemic: Ideas for Serving Your Community Anytime, Anywhere*, ed. Kathleen M. Hughes and Jamie Santoro (Chicago: American Library Association, 2021), 1–4.
2. Jill Barshay, "Proof Points: A Warning Sign That the Freshman Class Will Shrink Again in the Fall of 2021," *The Hechinger Report*, 2021, https://hechingerreport.org/warning-freshman-class-shrink-fall-2021.
3. "The Impact of COVID-19 on Entering Students in Community Colleges," Center for Community College Student Engagement, 2021, https://cccse.org/sites/default/files/SENSE_COVID.pdf.
4. Melissa Ezarik, "Student Experiences during COVID and Campus Reopening Concerns," *Inside Higher Ed*, March 24, 2021, www.insidehighered.com/news/2021/03/24/student-experiences-during-covid-and-campus-reopening-concerns.
5. Audrey Williams June, "For Community-College Students, It's Been a Tough Year," *Chronicle of Higher Education*, March 25, 2021, www.chronicle.com/article/for-community-college-students-its-been-a-tough-year.
6. Kansas Office of Rural Prosperity, "Broadband and Infrastructure," in "2020 ORP Annual Report," www.ruralkanprosper.ks.gov/wp-content/uploads/2021/02/Broadband-and-Infrastructure-Section.pdf.
7. Briley, "Fostering Social Connections," 1.
8. Ngox-Yen Tran and Silke Higgins, eds., *Supporting Today's Students in the Library* (Chicago: Association of College & Research Libraries, 2020).
9. Kaetrena D. Kendrick and Deborah Tritt, *The Small and Rural Academic Library* (Chicago: Association of College & Research Libraries, 2016).
10. Ty McNamee, Jenay Willis, Karen M. Ganss, Sonja Ardoin, and Vanessa A. Sansone, "Don't Forget About Rural Higher Education Students: Addressing Digital Inequities during COVID-19," *Diverse Issues in Higher Education* 37, no. 7 (2020).
11. McNamee et al., "Don't Forget About Rural Education Students," 12.
12. Micah M. Griffin, Beverly Kloeppel, and Giang T. Nguyen, "Introduction," in *Supporting Vulnerable Campus Populations during the COVID-19 Pandemic*, ed. Jean Chin (Silver Springs, MD: American College Health Association, 2020), 1–10.
13. Kendrick and Tritt, *The Small and Rural Academic Library*, 42.

SARAH SIMMS, NARCISSA HASKINS, AND EBONY MCDONALD

Together from the Ground Up

Deconstructing the Research Process for First-Semester Students at Louisiana State University

This chapter describes the efforts by a core team of three academic librarians at Louisiana State University (LSU) Libraries to support the course "HSS 1000: Introduction to Research" before and during the COVID-19 pandemic. This new College of Humanities and Social Sciences course was designed to support one of the most diverse cohorts of first-semester students in the university's history, one that was created by a shift in admissions policy in 2018.

Introduction

In 2018, Louisiana State University (LSU) implemented a holistic admissions approach, moving away from a reliance on standardized testing. Referred to as "comprehensive admissions," this new process recognizes prospective students for their potential beyond minimum standardized test scores. The measures for consideration include a student's high school transcript and curriculum, recommendation letters, personal essays, and extracurricular activities. This holistic approach was implemented to diversify the student body and increase enrollment.

The first class enrolled under comprehensive admissions was the largest and most diverse in LSU's history, and this positive trend has continued each year. These new cohorts include vulnerable populations that may be economically disadvantaged, first-generation, or from a historically underrepresented group, and often students are at the intersection of several of these described populations.

But admission is only the first step to support student success. Once enrolled, a student's success depends on a myriad of factors, including support systems and community networks. Jose Aviles, vice president for enrollment at LSU, captured this reality by stating that "our work doesn't stop once a student is admitted, though. LSU is increasing our retention and graduation rates. Each and every freshman admitted to LSU received personalized touch points from faculty and staff, and we offer all assistance available to ensure they are progressing toward graduation."[1] Those personalized touch points include specific courses created to help students transition to college.

Originating in the College of Humanities and Social Sciences (HSS), one such course is "HSS 1000: Introduction to Research." Created in 2018 as a requirement for all first-year HSS students to support that new and varied cohort of students, this semester-long one-hour course is a hybrid of a typical freshman seminar and an introduction to research in the humanities and social sciences. A portion of the course includes presentations by support services from around campus, while the other, often larger, portion focuses on research. Teaching librarians have a significant presence in the course, thus becoming even more involved in the early stages of the students' academic careers.

Responding to a Need through Collaboration

In HSS 1000's initial semester, the undergraduate and student success librarian, Sarah Simms, and other librarians from the Research and Instruction Services (RIS) Department of the university libraries were occasionally invited into classrooms with the goal of introducing research concepts, information literacy, and library resources. By their second semester, the popularity of the librarian-led classes had grown to the point of necessitating the creation of a three-librarian team to handle the bulk of requests from HSS 1000 instructors. This team consisted of Sarah Simms, Narcissa Haskins, the teaching and learning librarian, and Ebony McDonald, the African and African American studies diversity librarian, who was at that time in a three-month rotation in RIS.[2]

The library team's partnership with the instructors and rector of the HSS Residential College was especially important in planning the classes. Initially, the HSS Residential College was interested in a traditional demonstration of library resources and databases that this cohort of students would use as LSU students. But through a series of collaborative meetings, the librarian team demonstrated the depth and breadth of information literacy (IL) principles that could be introduced in the classroom and that would give greater meaning to using the library's resources. In effect, they planned to build a foundational knowledge of research, with the idea that additional library instruction would take place in higher-level classes, thereby creating a scaffolded instruction plan.

Teaching Styles and Techniques

With broad learning objectives in place, the core team of three librarians, each of whom had different levels of teaching experience and preferred teaching methods, prepared to teach these classes. Simms had five years of instruction experience, McDonald had two years of experience with instruction from her previous institution, and Haskins was a first-year librarian new to instruction who had just finished her onboarding at LSU Libraries.

Creating a core team to focus on a specific cohort of students enabled each librarian to contribute her specific strengths and expertise to the class. This assets-based approach led to the librarians leaning on and learning from each other, and in some cases co-teaching sections.

The following are three examples of teaching strategies used in these classes by each librarian.

Warmth-Based Instruction

First-semester students new to both a university setting and the concept of academic research may display a myriad of emotions: fear, shame, anxiety, indifference, and, in some cases, misplaced overconfidence. Their fears can be tied to a fear of failure, a competitive environment, and/or cultural factors.[3] Compounding this might be issues of library anxiety,[4] shame,[5] and anxieties stemming from the research process itself.[6] These fears and anxieties can negatively affect students' class participation and their ability to absorb the material: "the emotional attitudes that students bring to the learning situation strongly affect what and how much will be learned."[7] Beyond a classroom disposition, these same fears and anxieties can seriously hinder students' research efforts and can lead to procrastination. In an effort to combat this, we can use student-centered instruction that is mindful of "students' psychological barriers in an ever-changing information environment."[8]

One way to alleviate students' apprehensions is through warmth-based instruction—based on Mellon's warmth seminars—and by recognizing the emotional components surrounding the library, information-seeking, and research. Emotional warmth is a powerful tool, because "cognitively, people are more sensitive to warmth information than to competence information."[9] Simms used a combination of warmth-based instruction, personal narrative, and highlighting practical uses of the library resources, all underscored by her willingness and availability to help students throughout their journey: a teaching method that she has always employed in the classroom.

At the beginning of class, students answered questions about how the word "research" made them feel, and talked through exactly what it was about the research process which made them feel that way. Did they feel any apprehension about doing research? Finding a topic? Writing the paper that would be required in the course? Using citations? Were students excited at the prospect of researching a topic of actual personal interest to them? Were they eager to try their hand at searching the libraries' resources? The instructor and librarian would interject their own experiences with research: both good and bad. Creating an inclusive environment where the class reflected on and discussed their experiences with the library and the research process, including successes and failures, helped reduce students' anxieties at the outset of the instruction session. "Naming unspoken feelings opens the topic for discussion, and sharing uncomfortable feelings with others who can relate to the experience can be an effective way of diffusing the impact of these feelings. Moreover, correctly placing the root of the negative emotions within the process itself, rather than within the individual, allows students to experience the emotions in a less threatening and less personal way."[10] Due to this class exercise in shared experience and dialogue, the students came to understand that they were not alone in these feelings.

Another point of class discussion centered on the research process itself and misconceptions that it was a linear process. By dispelling the myth that research is linear, and by illustrating (at times literally) the complicated and labyrinthine nature of the iterative research process, Simms introduced, or in some cases reintroduced, the concept of research as an activity that is grounded in "authentic curiosity" and inquiry, as opposed to a reporting process.[11] Building upon this technique, our next discussion point centered on practical examples of finding research topics that would spark the students' personal interests.

The students discussed their experiences with the information cycle and the opportunities for discovering and developing topics outside of the "normal" channels of inspiration. We juxtaposed social media, blogs, and podcasts against newspapers, magazines, and even scholarly articles. Much consideration was given to introducing background research as a tool for students to learn about their topics and get to their actual research question. With these concepts in mind, the final twenty minutes of the class focused on basic search strategies using library resources.

At the end of the class, students again shared how they felt about the idea of research; through this oral self-reporting, tensions had decreased considerably while excitement about the prospect of future research had increased. By using classroom discourses based in warmth, authenticity, and vulnerability, we can create a space that nurtures knowledge creation, reflection, and the sharing of personal experiences, a valuable tool for connecting with our students and each other.

Mind Mapping

As an entry-level librarian, Haskins worked closely with Simms in the HSS 1000 classroom. During one of these seminars, she realized that adding another tool to the instruction process would boost student engagement and confidence.

Mind-mapping activities enable students to explore the connections within their primary topic area. Librarians have found it to be beneficial during IL sessions. For example, Cynthia Tysick taught graduate students to use mind mapping to brainstorm potential theses research.[12] In just fifteen minutes during the instruction, her students organized their concepts and variables. Tysick then took this practice further by integrating concept mapping. Unlike mind mapping, concept mapping narrows ideas and can even define the relationship between ideas within a central focus question.[13] Any form of mapping can prove beneficial during the beginning stages of the research process.

Though mind mapping within IL instruction has been used, it has not gained widespread use. Haskins found that some librarians at LSU Libraries still choose traditional instruction focusing on the library's resources and search methods. Furthermore, mind mapping, especially in the research process, is used as a multi-series experience. Haskins wanted to reimagine how functional mind mapping could be used in addition to her warmth-based method.

The ideal moment for mind mapping is right after discussing the information timeline with students. The information timeline shows students how information ages, and exposes how they can research their current interests. By this point in the instruction, the students have also discussed hot topics and why specific popular and scholarly sources are beneficial to their work. The students' engagement is noticeably active due to their anticipation of selecting a topic for their novice research projects.

Conducting quality research using library resources is a common source of insecurity and anxiety for first- and second-year students that runs rampant in the higher education environment. To combat these emotional responses, Haskins guided the class through the mind-mapping process by having the class pick a topic area and add to a collective mind map on the whiteboard. Mind mapping was crucial to the lesson because students tend to let their perceived lack of knowledge keep them from moving forward productively. Incorporating mind-mapping allows students to add to a collective body of work that temporarily relieves them from siloed, technology-driven work. Most importantly, it gives them a tool that enables them to find topic areas, narrow them, find crucial moments in the topics' history, and, most importantly, identify keywords for those topics.

This mind-mapping tool sets the stage for the background research process and allows the class to collectively participate in the research process and learn about sourcing pertinent information from both the internet and library databases.

Active Learning

Upon arriving at LSU and starting her three-month RIS rotation to support Simms and Haskins, McDonald had already developed her particular brand of IL library instruction. She had previous experience with and training on backward design methodology.[14] ACRL's *Framework for Informational Literacy for Higher Education* guided the content that she includes in her IL instructional design.[15] Her delivery methods rely heavily on active learning techniques.

In the HSS 1000 classes, McDonald (1) taught students to apply informal, "everyday" research skills to formal academic research by demonstrating similarities and differences between the two processes and appropriate resources; and (2) illustrated how useful library resources can be once the students understand how they are organized, especially in comparison to those everyday research resources. In her introduction to every lesson, McDonald provided examples of the "everyday" research she does and encouraged students to build upon their understanding of their own information-seeking behavior.

To help explain certain aspects of each lesson topic, McDonald embedded IL videos into dynamic slide presentations. The slides and subsequent informal assessment were designed to appeal to the different learning modalities.[16] She often chose search topics related to current events, such as the legalization of sex work or the use of hallucinogens to treat mental illness, and, using the same information timeline as Haskins and Simms, she showed how information is produced and that the available source types for their topics may depend on their currency.

To assess the lecture portions of the lesson, McDonald applied active learning techniques. Active learning is an educational method that encourages students to participate in the lesson beyond listening and note-taking. Rather than absorbing the lesson material passively, they are encouraged to engage with the material *actively*, often through personal inquiry or collaboration with each other. The goal of active learning is to build the critical thinking skills of the students through information analysis, synthesis, and/or evaluation.[17] One of the oldest (and perhaps best-known) active learning techniques is the Socratic method. Socrates instructed his students by introducing a problem as a question and then directing them in guided discussions about possible solutions.[18]

McDonald engaged students throughout her sessions with question-and-answer knowledge checks. Rather than raising their hands so that only a single student could answer, the activity allowed for all students to raise color-coded answer slips. Since the slips were color-coded, she could quickly measure the class's understanding of lesson topics, and students who were unsure of the answers could quickly learn from their classmates. She then called on a student or two to explain how they had made their determination. McDonald also emphasized that rather than trying to remember everything about the topics which she reviewed, the students' primary takeaway should be that there are knowledgeable librarians available to help them meet their diverse research needs. She intended for this statement to lessen any performance anxiety the students might have felt during the knowledge checks.

Teaching during COVID-19

By the 2020 fall semester, the library's services had pivoted to support the teaching methods employed in response to the COVID-19 pandemic. While some classes continued to meet in a reduced capacity in person, others were held virtually in an asynchronous or synchronous environment. The librarian team created a comprehensive research guide with online tutorials, videos, and guidance on the research process and library resources to support students enrolled in HSS 1000 regardless of the teaching modality. The research guide had potential as a teaching platform for librarians and a reference tool for students. The librarian-led classes had become integral to HSS 1000 by now, and the librarians continued to introduce research as they had previously, though now in a virtual environment.

The HSS Residential College rector oversees the welfare of students living in the HSS Residential College. In addition, the rector was tasked with teaching three sections of HSS 1000 and asked Simms and Haskins to visit each of these three sections twice, virtually, even though the students were attending in person. Having two class sessions allowed for deeper discussions about the research process. In the first session, discussions continued about what constitutes research, finding a topic, and identifying a "researchable" question. During the second session, Haskins used an online mind map to illustrate how students can engage with their current knowledge. In her example, students actively participated in creating the mind map by sharing their ideas and posing questions. The librarians also led discussions about evaluating sources and different evaluation techniques outside of the CRAAP model, such as the ACT UP technique created by Dawn Stahura.[19] By using a tool such as ACT UP, the librarians introduced the concept of privilege surrounding information and the academy.

While these classes were relatively successful, given the uncertainty due to the pandemic along with technical issues, student participation was not as involved as it had been in previous years. When faced with online instruction for these particular classes in the future, the continued use of the online mind map feature will be used in conjunction with both a flipped-classroom model and breakout rooms in an effort to prompt more participation from students.

Conclusion

In response to the COVID-19 pandemic, most colleges and universities in the United States not only reduced or waived application fees, but also moved to a test-optional or test-blind admissions process, effectively eliminating the SAT and ACT as a requirement for 2021–22 applicants. Because of their inherent racial and economic biases, these tests have historically been challenged as a barrier to entry into elite, predominately white institutions and a barrier to opportunities for students from traditionally underrepresented groups.[20]

Significant differences in test scores have been shown to exist between whites and minority groups in general.[21] While the College Board acknowledges the inequities in scores between groups, it defends the SAT and ACT tests as fair and claims that the scores are more a reflection of the unfairness within American society at large rather than in the tests themselves.[22] Lower test scores often lower the probability of receiving merit-based scholarships, which in turn can impact a family's ability to afford an elite college even if a student is accepted.[23] So, this monumental shift by academic institutions to eliminate these tests is seen as a long overdue step to achieving more equal opportunity for capable students of all socioeconomic backgrounds.

As expected, this unprecedented change has increased both the number of applications for institutions that have adopted this new policy and the diversity of applicants to the most competitive colleges and universities.[24] Colleges and universities are welcoming more African Americans, Latinos, Native Americans, and those from rural areas to their fall 2021 first-year student bodies, and many institutions will remain test-optional after the pandemic.[25] Considering the systemic disparities within K–12 education in the United States, these diverse new college students will matriculate into their first semester with differing levels of knowledge and skills, and these inequities will leave many students vulnerable to institutional cultures that have not been designed for them.[26]

For academic libraries, the questions then become: (1) how should librarians respond to the ever-increasing diversity of student bodies due to shifting admissions standards, and (2) how can librarians support the success of first-year students from high schools with inequitable teaching, technology, and support services?

As outlined in this chapter, Simms, Haskins, and McDonald rose to the challenge of responding to a new admissions policy that yields increased diversity among the first-year students. These librarians sought to understand and mitigate research anxiety in these students by using information literacy instruction that decentered expertise. Their methodologies leaned on both their individual teaching styles and the students' prior knowledge. Using their own unique techniques, they engaged in an asset-based rather than a deficit-based instruction model, which research has shown "increases student confidence and self-efficacy, and therefore, their ability to comprehend and retain new knowledge."[27] The asset-based model supports equity in education by benefiting from the talents that each student *and* instructor individually bring to the classroom experience.[28]

As we look at the future of IL instruction, the active participation of librarians in first-year seminars such as HSS 1000 is an important component in student learning and success through a "strategic and faculty-supported combination of direct instruction and assignment design consultation."[29] The HSS librarian team has a coveted seat at this table through its partnership with the HSS Residential College. They will continue to lend their expertise not only to various aspects of the research process, but to the creation of learning objectives and assignment designs related to this. While the course content may change, the teaching practices that this team of librarians use in the classroom will remain based in warmth, empathy, and connection through shared experiences. Their practices will continue to foster an environment of intentional conversations with students that nurtures creative approaches to future research possibilities.

NOTES

1. "LSU's New Admissions Model Already Showing Impressive Results," LSU Media Center. April 9, 2019, www.lsu.edu/mediacenter/news/2019/04/09 admissions.eb.php.
2. This particular team of librarians is racially diverse and included a first-generation college graduate. As such, each librarian brought different life experiences to the classroom that facilitated her connection and empathy with students across a broad spectrum. It is worth noting, however, that while the authors recognize the importance and need for diversity in all spheres of academia, the types of instruction and outreach described in this chapter are not dependent on diversity for success, but rather can be practiced by anyone regardless of identity.
3. Scott T. Bledsoe and Janice J. Baskin, "Recognizing Student Fear: The Elephant in the Classroom," *College Teaching* 62, no. 1 (2014): 32–34, https://doi.org/10.1080/87567555.2013.831022.
4. C. A. Mellon, "Library Anxiety: A Grounded Theory and Its Development," *College & Research Libraries* 47, no. 2 (1986): 160–65, https://doi.org/10.5860/crl_47_02_160.
5. Erin L. McAfee, "Shame: The Emotional Basis of Library Anxiety," *College and Research Libraries* 79, no. 2 (2018): 237–56, https://doi.org/10.5860/crl.79.2.237.
6. Carol C. Kuhlthau, "Inside the Search Process: Information Seeking from the User's Perspective," *Journal of the American Society for Information Science* 42, no. 5 (1991): 361–71; Carol C. Kuhlthau, *Seeking Meaning: A Process Approach to Library and Information Services*, 2nd ed. (Westport, CT: Libraries Unlimited, 2004).
7. Constance Mellon, "Attitudes: The Forgotten Dimension in Library Instruction," *Library Journal* 113, no. 14 (1988): 137–39, https://doi-org.libezp.lib.lsu.edu/10.1002/asi.10040.

8. Muhammad Asif Naveed, "Information-Seeking Anxiety: Background, Research, and Implications," *International Information & Library Review* 49, no. 4 (2017): 272, https://doi.org/10.1080/10572317.2017.1319713.
9. Susan T. Fiske, Amy J. C. Cuddy, and Peter Glick, "Universal Dimensions of Social Cognition: Warmth and Competence," *Trends in Cognitive Sciences* 11, no. 2 (2007): 78, https://doi.org/10.1016/j.tics.2006.11.005.
10. Jacqueline Kracker, "Research Anxiety and Students' Perceptions of Research: An Experiment. Part I: Effect of Teaching Kuhlthau's ISP Model," *Journal of the American Society for Information Science & Technology* 53, no. 4 (2002): 290, https://doi.org/10.1002/asi.10040.
11. Jean Donham, Jill A. Heinrich, and Kerry A. Bostwick, "Mental Models of Research: Generating Authentic Questions," *College Teaching* 58, no. 1 (2010): 8, https://doi.org/10.1080/87567550903263834.
12. Cynthia Tysick, "Concept Mapping and the Research Process: A Librarian's Perspective," *Proceedings of the First International Conference on Concept Mapping: Concept Maps: Theory, Methodology, Technology* 2 (2004): 365–68, http://cmc.ihmc.us/papers/cmc2004-020.pdf.
13. Crystal Renfro, "The Use of Visual Tools in the Academic Research Process: A Literature Review," *Journal of Academic Librarianship* 43, no. 2 (2017): 95–99, https://doi.org/10.1016/j.acalib.2017.02.004.
14. Grant P. Wiggins and Jay McTighe, *Understanding by Design*, expanded 2nd ed. (Alexandria, VA: Gale Virtual Reference Library, Association for Supervision and Curriculum Development, 2005).
15. Association of College & Research Libraries, *Framework for Information Literacy for Higher Education* (Chicago: American Library Association, 2015), www.ala.org/acrl/standards/ilframework.
16. VARK: A Guide to Learning Preferences, "The VARK Modalities," Vark Learn Limited, 2021, https://vark-learn.com/introduction-to-vark/the-vark-modalities.
17. Michael Lorenzen, "Active Learning and Library Instruction," *Illinois Libraries* 83, no. 2 (2001): 19–24.
18. Lorenzen, "Active Learning," 20.
19. Dawn Stahura, "ACT UP for Evaluating Sources: Pushing against Privilege," *College & Research Libraries News* 79, no. 10 (2018): 551, https://doi.org/10.5860/crln.79.10.551.
20. Nick Anderson, "More Students Applied to Top Colleges This Year: How Making Test Scores Optional Opened the Field," *The Washington Post*, April 5, 2021, www.washingtonpost.com/education/2021/04/05/college-admissions-2021-test-optional; Scott Jaschik, "New Evidence of Racial Bias on SAT," *Inside Higher Ed*, June 21, 2010, www.insidehighered.com/news/2010/06/21/new-evidence-racial-bias-sat; John Rosales and Tim Walker, "The Racist Beginnings of Standardized Testing," *NEA News*, National Education Association,

March 20, 2021, www.nea.org/advocating-for-change/new-from-nea/racist-beginnings-standardized-testing; Paul Tough and Ira Glass, "The Campus Tour Has Been Cancelled," produced by WBEZ, *This American Life*, March 19, 2021, podcast, MP3 audio, 00:59:17, www.thisamericanlife.org/734/the-campus-tour-has-been-cancelled.

21. FairTest, "SAT, ACT Bias Persist," National Center for Fair and Open Testing, n.d., www.fairtest.org/sat-act-bias-persist.

22. Jaschik, "New Evidence of Racial Bias." In 1926, the College Board administered the first Scholastic Aptitude Test (SAT), which they commissioned Carl Brigham, a psychologist and eugenicist, to develop. The desire to prove unequivocally the superiority of "the Nordic race group" through testing had guided Brigham in his previous work on intelligence tests for the U.S. Army and the publication of *A Study of American Intelligence* (1923). American College Testing (ACT) was developed in the 1950s (Rosales and Walker, "Racist Beginnings of Standardized Testing").

23. FairTest, "SAT, ACT Bias Persist"; Rosales and Walker, "Racist Beginnings of Standardized Testing."

24. Jack Jaschik, "Test-Optional Admissions Yields Benefits," *Inside Higher Ed*, April 19, 2021, www.insidehighered.com/admissions/article/2021/04/19/test-optional-colleges-get-more-pell-grant-students-minority-students.

25. Anderson, "More Students Applied to Top Colleges"; Tough and Glass, "Campus Tour Has Been Canceled."

26. Anderson, "More Students Applied to Top Colleges"; Jaschik, "Test-Optional Admissions"; Tough and Glass, "Campus Tour Has Been Canceled."

27. Tatiana Pashkova-Balkenhol, Mark Lenker, Emily Cox, and Elizabeth Kocevar-Weidinger, "Should We Flip the Script? A Literature Review of Deficit-Based Perspectives on First-Year Undergraduate Students' Information Literacy," *Journal of Information Literacy* 13, no. 2 (2019): 94.

28. Association of College & Research Libraries, "5 Things You Should Read about Asset-Based Teaching," American Library Association, 2018, https://acrl.ala.org/IS/wp-content/uploads/is-research_5Things_asset-based-teaching.pdf; Jackie Gerstein, "Approaching Marginalized Populations from an Asset Rather Than a Deficit Model of Education," Medium, May 19, 2021, https://medium.com/@jackiegerstein/approaching-marginalized-populations-from-an-asset-rather-than-a-deficit-model-of-education-d5bb05d256af; Janice D. Lombardi, "The Deficit Model Is Harming Your Students," Edutopia, June 14, 2016, www.edutopia.org/blog/deficit-model-is-harming-students-janice-lombardi; Lois Weiner, "Challenging Deficit Thinking," *Educational Leadership* 64, no. 1 (2006): 42–45.

29. Sara M. Lowe, Char Booth, Sean Stone, and Natalie Tagge, "Impacting Information Literacy Learning in First-Year Seminars: A Rubric-Based Evaluation," *portal: Libraries and the Academy* 15, no. 3 (2015): 500, doi:10.1353/pla.2015.0030.

ROSALIND FIELDER-GISCOMBE AND GABRIELLE TOTH

5

So Close and Yet So Remote

Using Technologies to Provide High-Touch, Personalized Support for Vulnerable Students

This chapter explores how reference librarians at Chicago State University's Gwendolyn Brooks Library (GBL) used best practices to support students as remote learners in response to the COVID-19 crisis. The librarians created new models for research assistance, shifting from predominantly on-campus, in-person reference services to remote online synchronous and asynchronous services. Along the way, we found ourselves serving student success by being one of the few units on campus to provide direct, face-to-face (although remote) service to students, giving them the human contact they needed academically and socially to feel connected to the institution and to their academic progress.

We begin with a brief discussion of the vulnerabilities among CSU students and the obstacles and difficulties a majority of them have been confronted with since the sudden shift to remote learning. Next, we review the literature on the roles that libraries and librarians play in student success, particularly among vulnerable students. The remainder of the chapter describes the new service models for research assistance that GBL reference librarians developed to support their students in a newly remote environment.

Background

At Chicago State, "vulnerable" students are simply students. CSU is the only four-year, predominantly Black institution of higher learning in Illinois.

About 68 percent of our students are African American, and another 10 percent are Hispanic. Our students' average age is 30, and 30 percent of our undergraduate students have dependents. About 55 percent are new transfer students. More than two-thirds of our students receive federal Pell grant funds. We are primarily a commuter campus serving a local population in a predominantly African American, predominantly low-income neighborhood on the South Side of Chicago.[1] The financial and work/life challenges faced by our adult learners and nontraditional student population are exceptional among college and university students.

When the COVID-19 pandemic necessitated the campus-wide shift to remote work and learning, we had students without access to computers and the internet, students charged with managing their own children's now-home-based remote learning, and students caring for family members who fell ill with COVID. Many of our students have been managing these responsibilities as full-time students while also working full-time or reeling from loss of employment due to COVID-19. While our institution worked hard to address the issues that it could, such as providing laptops and coordinating internet access for students in need, and offering COVID relief and emergency funding as appropriate, other hardships had no safe redress. Most CSU students had little interest in fully remote learning prior to the pandemic, but some were enrolled in online courses and programs pre-COVID as a means of making education fit into their busy schedules.

According to the Illinois Board of Higher Education, CSU's first-time, full-time freshman head count dropped by just over 20 percent from the 2019–20 academic year to the 2020–21 year. The new full-time transfer student head count was also down, by nearly 44 percent from 2019–20 to 2020–21. Full-time equivalent (FTE) enrollments among undergraduates dropped by 20 percent from 2019–20 to 2020–21.[2] This drop in FTEs may be an indicator of the hardships students faced due to COVID-19, leading them to enroll in fewer classes as their non-academic responsibilities changed or expanded. CSU undergraduate retention rates for fall 2019 students returning in fall 2020 dropped to 44 percent overall.[3] Given this data, the specter of students sitting out the COVID pandemic was real. This had serious consequences for our institution and for our students.

However, the remote services that GBL reference librarians provided ensured that our students had access to the library services they needed for their academic work. Recent literature on the subject of care ethics in librarianship, and the responses from CSU students we surveyed who participated in remote research consultations, suggest that the services we provided during this time helped make them feel that they were part of a campus experience, that they belonged, and that they could move forward. The dramatic shift to remote learning gave us the opportunity to transform our reference services so as to provide that high-touch experience which contributes significantly to the success of vulnerable students.

Prior to the shift to remote working, teaching, and learning in spring 2020, GBL's reference and instruction services to support online courses were fairly limited, due in large part to there being only two fully online programs offered at our institution, low demand from faculty and students, limited knowledge and experience within the librarian ranks, and insufficient personnel. But GBL reference librarians were determined to provide the same level, types, and quality of service our students deserve despite the impacts of the pandemic, so we immediately expanded our virtual reference and instruction services to include synchronous and asynchronous online library instruction, as well as live-online research consultations. By leveraging the available instructional technologies and cloud-based library applications, and by integrating web conferencing software newly acquired by our institution into our reference and instruction toolbox, we have been able to minimize the disruption to our students' education in the rapidly changing environment of the pandemic.

Literature Review

For nearly forty years, the literature on student success has included research into the role that students' feelings of belonging—as involvement, as engagement, as interaction, as community—play in student success, persistence, retention, and completion.[4] Over time, this literature has included the consideration of what supports success for "vulnerable" student populations. Schreiner built on the work of Astin, who decades ago identified campus involvement as being directly related to student learning and development, noting that her research revealed how race and social class made campus involvement harder for African American and Latino students. For African Americans, the obstacle was the number of hours they worked off-campus, more than other groups, and for Latinos, the obstacle was their commuter status.[5] Hausmann found that students' initial sense of belonging was associated with interactions with peers and with faculty, and with peer and parental support, but not with academic integration.[6] Later in their academic careers, students who reported more academic integration experienced an increase in their sense of belonging, while those with less academic integration felt a decrease in their sense of belonging.[7] Schreiner's study, which looked at the quality of student-faculty interactions, and not merely quantity, showed that for Latino students, these "strong social bonds and affirmations from faculty can make a significant difference." For African American students, when such interactions were positive, "not only did it lead directly to their thriving, but it also contributed to their sense of community on campus."[8] Bruce, citing Strayhorn and O'Keefe,[9] writes that a sense of belonging and connection with peers, faculty, and campus life are predictors of college success, and that students who feel that connection are more likely to achieve academic success, and graduate on time. By contrast, students who don't feel a sense of belonging perform poorly in and withdraw from classes, and delay completion of their degrees.[10]

Seminal research into libraries and student success over the past decade has demonstrated that libraries and librarians contribute to student success by contributing to higher rates of persistence and retention, and to better grades and GPAs; by adding value to students' long-term educational experience through library instruction; and by promoting academic rapport and student engagement.[11] The role of personal connection and empathy in providing library instruction to vulnerable student populations has been recognized in the library literature for at least thirty years, when Hall posited that personal rapport and maximizing contacts with students were more effective than "culturally congruent pedagogic models" in bibliographic instruction.[12] For Moreno and Jackson, writing nearly thirty years later, student success in the academic library is holistic, rooted in social justice, and is built on critical forms of librarianship "challenging the notion that libraries exist as neutral spaces."[13] When thinking about the role of librarians in student success, we must look beyond such measures of success as GPA or retention because they don't reflect "the larger story of students' experiences, particularly with regard to these experiences' emotional quality." The level of academic success depends on the quality of the support students are given, "including within the library."[14] Bruce applies theories of care ethics, relational-cultural theory, and critical race theory to the practice of individual research consultations to build a conceptual framework that demonstrates how these sessions contribute to students' feelings of connection and belonging by allowing librarians and students to forge relationships with each other. These relationships can lead to "transformational learning and teaching experiences" when they are free from the power structures that can make students feel inadequate, and when the relationships make the students feel seen. Bruce notes that Magi and Mardeusz[15] found that students who were frustrated in their research efforts "felt excited and prepared to continue their research" after the appointments. Quoting from their work, she writes: "In the same study, students expressed 'affective benefits including comfort, confidence-building, inspiration, and building relationships.'"[16]

New Service Models for Research Assistance

In mid-March 2020, the entire CSU campus shifted to remote learning and work because of the Illinois governor's statewide shutdown in response to the pandemic. During the extended spring break (two weeks) that immediately preceded the shift to remote learning, faculty members who had been teaching their courses on campus had to decide how they would provide instruction remotely. The overwhelming majority of teaching faculty had no prior experience teaching online and only limited experience using the university's course management system. GBL reference librarians were in a similar situation as teaching faculty. To meet the needs of an entire population of newly remote learners, most of whom had limited prior experience with online instruction and little enthusiasm for fully virtual education, we had to quickly establish the contours of our new service models, decide on delivery methods and the technologies we would use, and go about implementing our new fully remote reference and instruction services. The easiest decision to make was to provide unscheduled, live reference services via web form, text, e-mail, or chat using the Springshare LibAnswers platform, which we had long subscribed to, as a virtual reference desk. Continuity of unscheduled basic reference services was essential at a time when most campus services required an appointment. We also continued monitoring and responding to the department voicemail. We encouraged users, mostly students, who needed extensive assistance to initiate chat sessions with us so that we could launch Zoom sessions directly from chat. This allowed us to screen-share with users and simulate the face-to-face walk-up experience that users were accustomed to at our physical reference desk. Although most of the librarians at GBL were accustomed to using LibChat to engage with students virtually, none of us had used LibChat's Zoom integration prior to the shift to fully remote reference and instruction services.

Prior to the pandemic, most research consultations were handled in-person and on-the-fly at the reference desk by the scheduled librarian. Students preferring an appointment were also expected to come to the library. In rare instances, consultations were conducted by phone. From the outset of the pandemic, we added virtual research consultations via web-conferencing software to our reference services via the individual Zoom and GoToMeeting accounts made available to all faculty, including librarians. By claiming both accounts, we had the flexibility to use the software an individual student was most familiar with. Using web-conferencing software to share screens for virtual research consultations was a monumental service enhancement. Enabling a student to control our own mouse and keyboard remotely using that software facilitated active learning. Librarians offered students the option of having the session recorded, which would allow students to engage more fully, and the shared recording was also useful for review. Our new virtual research consultation model has been a game changer. We launched a web-based appointment request system to facilitate, centralize, and formalize appointment requests, and distribute assignments. We used the form to gather the information we would collect during a reference interview, as well as a range of data to inform our service decisions and marketing efforts. A key component of the process was optimum flexibility. Students could submit their request anytime from anywhere without human intervention. They could indicate up to three preferred dates/times for an appointment.

All reference faculty received a copy of each request, ensuring that none would fall through the cracks. Requests were also channeled through a dashboard, enabling us to claim specific requests so as to avoid duplicate effort.

So Remote and Yet So Close

To determine the effectiveness of our remote research consultations in promoting student learning and student success at CSU, we conducted a web-based anonymous survey. We were seeking to determine whether the virtual high-touch experience and live-human interactions we were able to provide to students helped them not only academically, but also helped them feel like they were a part of university life, even as the pandemic forced CSU to reduce or eliminate physical presence on campus. These questions are significant because the research referenced in the literature review suggests that two key factors in the success and the persistence, retention, and completion rates of all students, particularly of nontraditional students, are working with librarians and feeling as if they "belong" at the institution. We used the survey to collect data relevant to both principles. The survey participants were students who participated in at least one virtual research consultation with a GBL reference librarian during the spring 2020, fall 2020, or spring 2021 semesters. Most potential participants were undergraduate students, and the balance were graduate students. The students answered a broad range of questions. The questions most salient to the current discussion were attitudinal in nature. Participants rated their research consultation experience, and they answered questions aimed at establishing whether a connection exists between direct, live assistance from a librarian and student success. The survey responses received thus far suggest that GBL reference librarians had a positive impact on student success even though our interactions were remote. They contributed to the students' sense that they "belonged" to the university, and helped them continue to feel connected. In response to the statement, "Working with a librarian helped me to feel more confident that I would succeed in school in spite of the pandemic," 53 percent of students replied that they either somewhat agreed or strongly agreed. The response was even stronger to the statement, "Live, online assistance from the librarian contributed to my successful completion of the course." More than 82 percent of students indicated that they either somewhat agreed or strongly agreed. Regarding the matter of belonging or connectedness, 70 percent of students either somewhat agreed or strongly agreed with the statement, "Live, online assistance from the librarian made me feel more connected to the University"; 47 percent strongly agreed with this statement.

Conclusion

GBL reference librarians established and implemented new models of virtual reference services in the middle of an academic term and amid a pandemic to provide continuity of real-time, direct service to students who were newly engaged in remote learning. In doing so, we directly contributed to students' success despite new barriers to degree completion, and to students' sense of connection to the university. The services that we initially established or transformed to meet a particular moment can easily be sustained as distance library services that we had long envisioned but didn't realize we already had the technical capacity to implement. By maintaining these services after faculty and students return to campus, we have positioned ourselves to effectively meet our students wherever they are rather than where we are, physically and figuratively. We have not only expanded our capacity to support students in online programs, or enrolled in online courses, in a significant way, but we have also reduced the necessity of *any* student making a special trip to campus for assistance from a reference librarian. The latter is particularly significant because we are predominantly a commuter campus, and are located in one of the largest metropolitan areas in the country. Finally, we have broadened and deepened our professional experience with instructional and other information technologies. We have also identified gaps in our professional development to address, and can thus further enhance our ability to contribute to student success.

NOTES

1. "2020 Annual Report," 13, Chicago State University, www.flipsnack.com/ChicagoState/chicago-state-university-2020-annual-report.html.
2. "IBHE First Look Fall Enrollment 2020," Illinois Board of Higher Education, www.ibhe.org/First-Look-Fall-Enrollment-2020.html.

3. "Student Achievement, 2021," Chicago State University, Office of Institutional Effectiveness and Research, www.csu.edu/IER/student_achievement.htm.

4. Alexander W. Astin, "Student Involvement: A Developmental Theory for Higher Education," *Journal of College Student Personnel* 25 (1984): 297–308; Alexander W. Astin, What Matters in College? Four Critical Years Revisited (San Francisco: Jossey-Bass, 1993); John P. Bean, "Dropouts and Turnover: The Synthesis and Test of a Causal Model of Student Attrition," *Research in Higher Education* 12, no. 2 (1980): 155–87; John P. Bean, "Interaction Effects Based on Class Level in an Explanatory Model of College Student Dropout Syndrome," *American Educational Research Journal* 22, no. 1 (1985): 35–64, https://doi.org/10.2307/1162986; Darnell Cole, "Do Interracial Interactions Matter? An Examination of Student-Faculty Contact and Intellectual Self-Concept," *Journal of Higher Education* 78, no. 3 (2007): 249–81, https://doi.org/10.1353/jhe.2007.0015; Shevawn B. Eaton and John P. Bean, "An Approach/Avoidance Behavioral Model of College Student Attrition," *Research in Higher Education* 36, no. 6 (1995): 617–45; Sylvia Hurtado and Deborah Faye Carter, "Effects of College Transition and Perceptions of the Campus Racial Climate on Latino College Students' Sense of Belonging," *Sociology of Education:* 70, no. 4 (1997): 324–45, https://doi.org/10.2307/2673270; Carol A. Lundberg and Laurie Schreiner, "Quality and Frequency of Faculty-Student Interaction as Predictors of Learning: An Analysis by Student Race/Ethnicity," *Journal of College Student Development* 45, no. 5 (2004): 549–65, https://doi.org/10.1353/csd.2004.0061; Ernest T. Pascarella and Patrick T. Terenzini, *How College Affects Students: Findings and Insights from Twenty Years of Research* (San Francisco: Jossey-Bass, 1991); Ernest T. Pascarella and Patrick T. Terenzini, *How College Affects Students: A Third Decade of Research* (San Francisco: Jossey-Bass, 2005); Vincent Tinto, *Leaving College: Rethinking the Causes and Cures of Student Attrition*, 2nd ed. (Chicago: University of Chicago Press, 1993); Claude M. Steele, "A Threat in the Air: How Stereotypes Shape Intellectual Identity and Performance," *American Psychologist* 52 (1997): 613–29; Terrell L. Strayhorn, *College Students' Sense of Belonging: A Key to Educational Success for All Students* (New York: Routledge, 2012).

5. Laurie A. Schreiner, "Different Pathways to Thriving among Students of Color: An Untapped Opportunity for Success," *About Campus: Enriching the Student Learning Experience* 19, no. 5 (November–December 2014): 12, https://doi.org/10.1002/abc.21169.

6. Leslie R. M. Hausmann, Janet Ward Schofield, and Rochelle L. Woods, "Sense of Belonging as a Predictor of Intentions to Persist among African American and White First-Year College Students," *Research in Higher Education* 48, no. 7 (2007): 824, https://doi.org/10.1007/s11162-007-9052-9.

7. Hausmann et al., "Sense of Belonging," 824.

8. Schreiner, "Different Pathways," 14.

9. Symphony Bruce, "Teaching with Care: A Relational Approach to Individual Research Consultations," In the Library with the Lead Pipe, February 5, 2020, www.inthelibrarywiththeleadpipe.org/2020/teaching-with-care; Strayhorn, College Students' Sense of Belonging; Patrick O'Keefe, "A Sense of Belonging: Improving Student Retention," *College Student Journal* 47, no. 4 (2013): 605–13.

10. Bruce, "Teaching with Care."

11. Megan Oakleaf and Association of College & Research Libraries, *Value of Academic Libraries: A Comprehensive Research Review and Report* (Chicago: Association of College & Research Libraries, 2010), www.ala.org/acrl/sites/ala.org.acrl/files/content/issues/value/val_report.pdf; Karen Brown, Kara J. Malenfant, and Association of College & Research Libraries, *Academic Library Impact on Student Learning and Success: Documented Practices from the Field* (Chicago: Association of College & Research Libraries, 2015), www.ala.org/acrl/sites/ala.org.acrl/files/content/issues/value/contributions_report.pdf; Karen Brown, Kara J. Malenfant, and Association of College & Research Libraries, *Academic Library Impact on Student Learning and Success: Findings from Assessment in Action Team Projects* (Chicago: Association of College & Research Libraries, 2017), www.ala.org/acrl/sites/ala.org.acrl/files/content/issues/value/findings_y3.pdf; Karen Brown, Kara J. Malenfant, and Association of College & Research Libraries, *Documented Library Contributions to Student Learning and Success: Building Evidence with Team-Based Assessment in Action Campus Projects* (Chicago: Association of College & Research Libraries, 2016), www.ala.org/acrl/sites/ala.org.acrl/files/content/issues/value/contributions_y2.pdf.

12. Patrick Andrew Hall, "The Role of Affectivity in Instructing People of Color: Some Implications for Bibliographic Instruction," *Library Trends* 39, no. 3 (1991): 317.

13. Teresa Helena Moreno and Jennifer M. Jackson, "Redefining Student Success in the Academic Library: Building a Critically Engaged Undergraduate Engagement Program," *Research Library Issues*, no. 301 (March 2020): 8, https://doi.org/10.29242/rli.301.2.

14. Moreno and Jackson, "Redefining Student Success," 10, 15.

15. Trina Magi and Patricia E. Mardeusz, "Why Some Students Continue to Value Individual, Face-to-Face Research Consultations in a Technology-Rich World," *College & Research Libraries* 74, no. 6 (2013): 605–18, https://doi.org/10.5860/crl12-363.

16. Bruce, "Teaching with Care"; Magi and Mardeusz, "Why Some Students," 612.

JENNIFER MATTHEWS AND DEBORAH GASPAR

Reenvisioning Learning in a Time of Disruption

Rowan University is a public institution in southern New Jersey serving 19,600 students. The university offers more than 130 undergraduate, graduate, and doctoral degree programs across three campuses located in both urban and suburban communities. Rowan University Libraries (RUL) consists of three libraries: Campbell Library, the university's main academic library, in Glassboro; Cooper Medical School of Rowan University (CMSRU) Library, an academic medical library within Cooper University Hospital in Camden; and the Rowan School of Osteopathic Medicine (SOM) Health Sciences Library, a second academic medical library in Stratford.

As a rapidly growing university in an area of New Jersey that was formerly largely farmland, Rowan is now shifting toward industry and public health institutions. The student population includes 34.4 percent minority students, with 11.4 percent of the population identifying as Hispanic and nearly 10 percent as African American. This rich diversity creates a healthy, integrated campus life, but the interruption of COVID-19 has highlighted another category of diversity that may be a by-product of race and ethnicity: economic stratification.

The complications arising from COVID-19 exacerbated concerns that Rowan had already identified. The university has worked aggressively to address issues related to food insecurity and housing and has actively sought to provide affordable education. In 2016, representatives from departments across campus met to form the Affordability Task Force. The library has had a long-standing role in this task force through its ongoing collaboration with partners across campus. Librarians partnering with this task force provide the faculty with education on open educational resources (OER) and open access (OA) materials. The library was instrumental in the design and funding of the Textbook Alternative Program (TAP), which provides stipends to faculty members who redesign their course to use open education textbooks or course packets using subscribed materials through the library. A current "faculty learning community" series is focused on OER benefits, writing, and repositories of resources.

Remote Learning via Library Workshops

The quick transition to remote learning in March 2020 tasked instructors with a new and, in many cases, unfamiliar format for teaching. This, coupled with students' stress regarding the pandemic, led to disengagement and interruptions to student learning.

The Rowan Libraries are ever ready to partner with faculty to support students and have provided in-person workshops for the campus communities for many years. The pandemic-induced pivot to remote learning furnished a forced opportunity for librarians to reenvision their offerings to the university. Librarians quickly shifted their usual in-person workshops to free virtual workshops with a wide range of time slots to accommodate faculty, staff, and students. The workshops were offered on four topics: digital research tools, evaluating information in the digital age, scholarly communication, and citation management. Interest and attendance in this new format have increased exponentially since spring 2020, when only three workshops were offered to the campus community. Since the onset of the pandemic, the workshop offerings have expanded to 23 in fall 2020 and 36 in spring 2021. The workshop series also includes one hosted by a faculty member from the Department of Geography, Planning, and Sustainability who led a discussion of GIS software. This partnership with a faculty member to offer a workshop hosted by the library is one that Rowan Libraries hopes to encourage in the months and years to come. Recordings and elements for some workshops have been made available asynchronously.

The development of these new virtual workshops had multiple benefits. First, they allowed the students to continue to remotely access the wide-ranging topics as needed. Second, these workshops enabled the faculty and staff to continue to participate in them for their own professional development.

Additionally, faculty and library staff learned alongside students and could witness where students needed additional instruction in information literacy. The libraries developed a variety of workshops so as to allow everyone, from beginning undergraduate students to faculty members and university staff, to attend regardless of varying levels of expertise. By conducting joint workshops that are not segregated into student-only or faculty-only, the university community can identify more readily where its members' collective skills and knowledge lie.

Librarians also serve as critical partners in faculty learning communities (FLC), where they collaborate with faculty and other university staff members to organize workshops that focus on defined issues that may assist classroom learning across campuses. The FLC, too, moved into an online format and built on the library workshops that are offered to students.

As defined by DuFour et al., faculty learning communities "operate under the assumption that the key to improved learning for students is continuous, job-embedded learning for educators."[1] The "key" that DuFour et al. refer to is continuous learning and collective inquiry. Through collective inquiry, the university faculty work together to ensure that the students acquire the skills and knowledge that have been laid out as expectations for each course and degree program. Cuddapah and Clayton discuss in their study how the development of faculty learning communities aids in the apprenticing of those new to the community. Through the development of such a community, a practice of shared enterprises can be developed which can "sustain mutual engagement in action."[2] These learning communities consist of discussions and include mentoring and learning for all participants so that members are involved in discussions which Wenger, in his Communities of Practice, identified as focusing on five areas: self-relation to students, teacher roles, becoming a teacher, self-assessment, and revealing a conflicted self.[3]

Since Rowan University's administration has preferred electronic resources for many years now, the quick pivot to electronic support for courses at the onset of the COVID-19 pandemic was achievable for the university libraries. The transition of workshops, whether those offered for the entire university community or for the faculty-focused FLC, to a virtual model now brings library learning sessions in line with library resources that support research and curricula. It is likely that the university will continue this emphasis on remote learning. Therefore, the libraries are continually seeking to improve and expand the electronic offerings (both resources and learning opportunities) available to faculty and students.

New Student Success Partnerships

An exciting new partnership has developed as a result of the COVID-19 pandemic. One of the three Rowan University Libraries is Campbell Library on the main campus in Glassboro, New Jersey. This library is now actively collaborating with three other university units to strengthen students' awareness of the academic support services available to them, and to deliver those services in concert with each other. The initial collaboration was on a series of programs titled "Upgrade Your Grade." Unlike the workshops provided by the libraries that target the entire university community or just faculty, these sessions are designed specifically for students. This initiative grew out of student needs that various campus partners were unable to effectively address in COVID-related isolation. Much of the initial impetus for this partnership resulted from research being conducted by a graduate student and library employee who was studying how the library impacts student retention.

Campbell Library, the Writing Center, academic coaching, and tutoring are now promoting their complementary services as a suite of services for student success. Each of these services faced challenges with the quick shift to remote learning in March 2020, and the resulting issues emphasized that the services were segregated and isolated from each other rather than complementary and coordinated to effectively meet student needs.

The transition to remote learning was particularly challenging for neurodiverse students, many of whom rely on one or more of the academic support services even if they were unaware of the other services available to them. Rowan University offers robust support for more than 2,000 students who have registered for disability support services. The professional staff who lead the tutoring and coaching services were particularly concerned about those students, and they recognized that the students were often unaware of the other isolated services.

All the partners bring unique services to the collective suite. Academic coaching targets skills such as prioritization, time management, and communicating with instructors. Tutoring covers the range of basic course topics such as chemistry, calculus, and languages. Librarians concentrate on information literacy, with the location and selection of materials as a focus. The Writing Center supports students through outlines, early drafts, and final proofing. But these services are only effective when students are aware of them and understand how to reach out for assistance.

It is important to note that there has not been a shared physical space for these services either. Academic coaching and tutoring compete for space in one building, and the Writing Center is on the first floor of the Campbell Library building. Referring students between these departments has resulted in confusion for students, who often failed to follow up referrals, even when it would have been to their benefit. Even though the Writing Center is located in Campbell Library, the hand-off between services involves physical barriers as well. The reference and research librarians are on the second floor, but the main service desk for basic reference and circulation is on the first floor. Students are more likely to stop at the first-floor desk for assistance because it is quick and obvious.

The staff reviewed a bibliography of articles related to student retention and service partnerships. As the partnership formed, much like those outlined in Raspa and Ward's *The Collaborative Imperative*,[4] it became clear to each member that actively building a network to support student needs would benefit not only students but the staff working with them. S. Bell notes that "when librarians become part of a student's support network, the student improves in ways that lead to better academic performance."[5] Eng and Stadler assert that "no single provider retains a monopoly on a student's college education, but rather what really matters is if the student graduates."[6]

The partners also established the primary goal of their collaboration: to strengthen students' awareness of academic support services. Representatives from each service met regularly to discuss shared communication and outreach strategies. As noted, there is no shared physical space for students' academic services, so the representatives moved forward on a shared virtual space necessitated by remote work and classes.

Planning for an online series of workshops started during the fall 2020 semester, and the inaugural series of Upgrade Your Grade programming ran through the 2021 spring semester to meet the shifting needs of students.

The spring workshops were all presented online, with follow-up messages to the attendees. Though a small number of students lived on campus, classes were still fully online, and it was determined that offering this pilot series of workshops in a hybrid format would be confusing.

The first session in the series was titled "Planning Your Semester" and was facilitated by a student tutor who led a panel discussion which introduced academic services to the students who logged in. The participating students were invited to ask questions and verify which service or services would best meet their needs. Representatives from the four services spoke with the attendees about what a student could expect when meeting with their staff. They also carefully explained how to make one-on-one appointments and what the student could prepare beforehand in order to make the time together more productive.

It was during this session that the value of the new collaboration became even more evident. The reference librarian, tutor, Writing Center director, and academic coach each stressed the need for the students to actively plan for the sessions. They noted that the sessions would be more effective if students brought their assignment or writing prompt to work with others. The shared message was of professional support but student responsibility.

The next session followed a few weeks later and targeted midterm exams and mid-semester assignments. This was also synchronized with the national "Night Against Procrastination" program. Students who joined this session received an introduction to the various academic services, and then visited breakout rooms in Zoom to work with tutors, Writing Center staff, coaches, or librarians. Several of the students moved between breakout rooms to better understand who would best meet their needs. The Night Against Procrastination program was not as effective online as it would have been in person. This was not a surprise to the partners, as it is hard to foster a sense of community in Zoom. The online format hindered engagement and attendance. The partners also acknowledged that students are weary of online class meetings, whether by Zoom, Webex, or Google Meets. Consequently, the Upgrade Your Grade programs during the fall 2021 semester were focused on using spaces in the Campbell Library.

The last session of the spring series was titled "Prep for Finals!" and was presented online two weeks before final exams. This session was advertised as time for a final preparation of papers and projects, as well as strategies for studying for final exams. The participating students were invited to ask questions and share strategies that have worked for them. Each service representative provided information about hours and what students could expect from end-of-the-semester services. The representatives also gave quick tips about studying, capitalizing on instructor office hours, and finding the right study space.

The shared commitment to this new academic support group has earned administrative support. The dean of the Ric Edelman College of Communication and Creative Arts, the associate provost for libraries and information, and the vice president of student affairs have met to endorse the ongoing work of the group.

An exciting development is that university administrators have endorsed designating a shared service hub for students in the library. As of this writing, the service hub has been written into the university's strategic goals. Space planning, together with infrastructure planning, are scheduled to begin in December 2021.

Conclusion

The COVID-19 pandemic provided Rowan University librarians with a forced opportunity to reframe their existing services and to expand existing partnerships while also fostering new ones. The initial transition to solely online instruction and services highlighted the limitations of siloed services both in the library and in other units across campus. It also documented that students, whether on campus or studying remotely, didn't know about the academic support services that are available to them. Many students struggled with the abrupt transition to online learning and would have benefited from using the support system designed by the university.

Though the library's collection and infrastructure were already positioned for full online access, instruction sessions and workshops were not. The librarians have been working on a robust set of asynchronous workshops and learning modules while still offering synchronous information literacy sessions. This variety makes these services more convenient and, therefore, more attractive to faculty and students who are also working remotely.

NOTES

1. *Doing: A Handbook for Professional Learning Communities at Work* (Bloomington, IN: Solution Tree, 2016), 10.
2. Jennifer L. Cuddapah and Christine D. Clayton, "Using Wenger's Communities of Practice to Explore a New Teacher Cohort," *Journal of Teacher Education* 62, no. 1 (2011): 62–75, https://doi.org/10.1177/0022487110377507.
3. Etienne Wenger, *Communities of Practice: Learning, Meaning, and Identity* (Cambridge: Cambridge University Press, 1998).
4. Dick Raspa and Dane Ward, *The Collaborative Imperative: Librarians and Faculty Working Together in the Information Universe* (Chicago: Association of College & Research Libraries, 2000).
5. S. J. Bell, "Retention Matters, But It's Not the Only Thing That Counts," *Information Outlook* 1, no. 18 (2014): 11–14, https://scholarworks.sjsu.edu/sla_io_2014/1.
6. S. Eng and D. Stadler, "Linking Library to Student Retention: A Statistical Analysis," *Evidence Based Library and Information Practice* 10, no. 3 (2015): 50–63, https://doi.org/10.18438/B84P4D.

Part II

Programming That Fosters Inclusion

KRISTINA CLEMENT

Information Privilege and First-Generation Students

A Librarian-in-Residence Program to Facilitate Information Access at the University of Wyoming

There are several definitions of the term *information privilege* in the field of librarianship, and though they may differ, they all center around one theme: access to information. The term *information privilege* was defined by Char Booth (and first coined by Booth in 2013) as the unequal access to information, with "'privilege' [defined] as the advantages, opportunities, rights, and affordances granted by status and positionality via class, race, gender, culture, sexuality, occupation, institutional affiliation, and political perspective."[1] Others have sought to provide definitions that focus on specific intersections of information privilege, such as information privilege and information literacy, information privilege and open access, and information privilege and assumptions of power.[2]

How we access information can depend greatly on how privileged we are. For several decades now, the "digital divide" has been discussed as one of the primary causes of imbalance between the information "haves" and the information "have-nots."[3] This is especially true for regions with significant rural populations who often lack access to high-speed internet, like the state of Wyoming. When it comes to information privilege and access to information, Wyoming is in a unique position as the least populated state in the United States, with fewer than 600,000 residents. Many residents live in rural communities and their access to information is not necessarily guaranteed; "about 45 percent of Wyoming residents [who live] in areas designated as rural by the U.S. Census Bureau don't have access to high speed [internet] service, compared to only 2 percent in urban areas."[4] In their news article, Schmelzer and Peterson link to the Federal Communications Commission's Fixed Broadband Deployment map for the state of Wyoming, which makes it clear that there are significantly fewer providers which are able to provide broadband access that meets the federal speed standards of 25 megabits per second (Mbps) for download and 3 Mbps for upload,[5] and that rural areas of the state are unequally affected.

One population at the University of Wyoming (UW) which can be disproportionately affected by the lack of access to information in rural areas of the state is first-generation students. Between 30 and 40 percent of enrolled students at the University of Wyoming are considered first-generation; the University of Wyoming defines a first-generation student as someone whose parents did not complete a college degree.[6] Close to 70 percent of UW students are residents of the state of Wyoming, with many coming from rural communities. Therefore, first-generation rural students are potentially moving from positions of less information privilege (lack of reliable internet, smaller secondary school systems, lack of access to a nearby institution of higher education, etc.) to significantly more information privilege when they become university students (more reliable internet access, access to university library resources, access to university faculty)—potentially more so than their continuing generation classmates (whether rural or not). One way of visualizing the transfer of information privilege that students may encounter in their transition from high school to college is shown in figure 7.1, which illustrates the various information privileges that students may have in high school and then later in college. This graphic has been used in college and university information literacy instruction sessions across the United States to help students think critically about their own privilege, power, and what it means to have access to information as a college student. The graphic is an adaptation inspired by Peggy McIntosh's 1989 essay "White Privilege: Unpacking the Invisible Knapsack,"[7] which centers primarily on the privileges afforded to those based on their race. This particular adaptation does not necessarily factor in race into the list of privileges afforded students in high school and college, but rather takes the concept of the "invisible knapsack" and applies it to the types of information privilege that high school and college students may or may not have.

CHAPTER 7: INFORMATION PRIVILEGE AND FIRST-GENERATION STUDENTS / 73

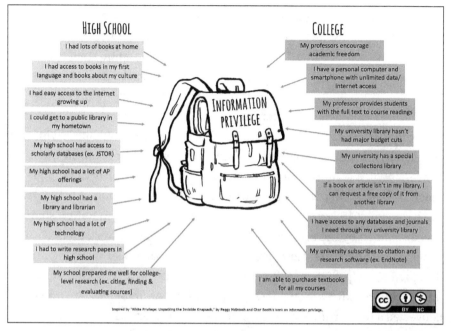

FIGURE 7.1
Invisible Knapsack

Duke University Libraries, "Invisible Knapsack," graphic inspired by Peggy McIntosh's 1989 essay "White Privilege: Unpacking the Invisible Knapsack." Knapsack graphic by Amelia Rozear.

Because this graphic was originally created in an urban part of the United States, the privileges listed in high school are not necessarily the same for high school students in rural Wyoming. The privileges listed in college, however, accurately reflect what students have access to when they start their academic careers at the University of Wyoming. This sudden influx of access to information can be overwhelming, especially for first-generation students from rural communities.

Library Outreach to First-Generation Students

While there is a wealth of literature about library outreach and engagement efforts, there is far less written about outreach specifically to first-generation students, with much of the current literature having been published in the last several years. There are several authors who discuss designing services and outreach models with first-generation students in mind, and much of their programming originates from the intersection between library anxiety and information literacy.[8] As Arch and Gilman note, "libraries have a unique opportunity, and a responsibility, to support first-generation students as they progress through their education. Libraries must ensure their services and resources are helping students navigate their academic requirement, not presenting a challenge as other institutional structures do."[9] The University of Wyoming has several resources for first-generation students,[10] with new programs and resources added regularly. However, prior to spring 2019, the University of Wyoming Libraries had very few resources, services, and outreach programs that were targeted specifically to this group of students. In the spring of 2019, a new peer-mentor program for first-generation students was developed by the university's Learning Resource Network (LeaRN). This program is called First Gen Scholars and serves as a peer-mentor program designed to help first-year, first-generation students at UW connect to the university's resources, activities, and programs. Additionally, the university converted a former sorority house into a small residence hall to house a community of sixty-seven first-generation students beginning in fall 2019. All the resident assistants (RAs) in the newly named Tobin House are also first-generation students, typically juniors and seniors, who regularly plan specialized events and programming tailored for the residents. In order to find ways to keep up with these exciting developments for first-generation students, the student success librarian began to consider ways for the UW Libraries to better include and serve first-generation students while also addressing information privilege, access to information, and rural communities.

Library Support for First-Generation Students

The First Gen Scholars program launch provided an opportunity for new library outreach to first-generation students. The UW Libraries' successful Personal Librarian Program (PLP) for transfer students and veterans served as a foundation for first-generation student outreach. However, the new outreach would consist of more in-person communication than the e-mail-based PLP, in order to create an inclusive environment and convey to the first-generation students their important place in the campus community. Discussions between the director of the First Gen Scholars program and the student success librarian resulted in the idea of providing on-site library assistance at Tobin House; this is similar to the concept of pop-up libraries, which are fairly common at many colleges and universities. One of the major goals of this outreach initiative would be to bring information access directly to where a focused group of first-generation students live and spend a significant amount of their time—their residence hall. A partnership was formed between the UW Libraries, the First Gen Scholars program director, and the Tobin House resident coordinator to develop effective strategies for the initiative, the Librarian-in-Residence program.

Librarian-in-Residence

The Librarian-in-Residence program came into existence in the fall of 2019. However, before the program launched, there were a number of logistical considerations that the UW Libraries and the Tobin House resident coordinator had to agree upon.

Participation

When designing the Librarian-in-Residence program for Tobin House, one of the major considerations was identifying stakeholders beyond the student success librarian. The program ultimately launched with only the student success librarian hosting hours at Tobin House. This was to ensure that Tobin House residents had a single point of contact for library help within their living space. There was concern that having multiple librarians visit the house weekly would cause confusion about whom to contact with library-related questions. Having all contact funnel through the student success librarian streamlined referrals, and the residents got used to having a librarian present in their living space. There are plans for discussions about an additional librarian presence in Tobin House once the COVID-19 pandemic has passed.

Frequency, Duration, Access, and Location

Some of the most important logistical considerations for making the Librarian-in-Residence program a success were (1) how often the student success librarian would go to Tobin House; (2) how long the librarian would stay at the house; and (3) how the librarian would access the house. The scheduled times, which were two-hour blocks, twice a week, took into consideration when classes typically started and finished, and provided both a morning time and an afternoon time to accommodate student preferences. Additionally, the student success librarian needed to secure card swipe access to Tobin House in order to successfully provide in-residence library services. Tobin House is accessible to residents only by card swipe, and guests must be accompanied by a resident. Having a librarian-in-residence there was a new concept, and it took longer than expected to secure access and permission for the student success librarian. The residence coordinator worked with the director of Residence Life and Dining Services to grant card swipe access to the librarian for the days and times that she would be in Tobin House. The last logistical consideration was selecting an appropriate place for library consultations. Tobin House is a converted sorority house that has four common areas on the main level (living room, kitchen, TV room, and game room), dorm rooms and reading nooks on the second and third floors, and a resident advisor's office and mailroom on the main level. The student success librarian held her library hours in Tobin House in the common areas where students spent time between classes.

Assistance and Publicity

Once the schedule was set and access was granted, the student success librarian set parameters for the types of assistance she would offer to Tobin House residents. This ensured that she was adequately facilitating inclusive access to all of the information that university students have, while also defining boundaries and referral procedures to connect students to non-library-related resources when needed. The librarian-in-residence would be available to help with requests related to library resources, services, spaces, experts, and basic IT assistance. Anything else would be referred to the appropriate student unit or academic office. A variety of flyers communicated to first-generation students when and where they could receive assistance from the librarian-in-residence. Figure 7.2 shows the flyer that was provided to students during the fall 2019 move-in, and figure 7.3 shows the sign that was displayed each time the student success librarian was at Tobin House. The Tobin House web page on the university's "Housing & Residence Life" website also advertised the Librarian-in-Residence service.

CHAPTER 7: INFORMATION PRIVILEGE AND FIRST-GENERATION STUDENTS / 77

FIGURE 7.2
Flyer that was distributed to Tobin House residents at move-in, fall 2019

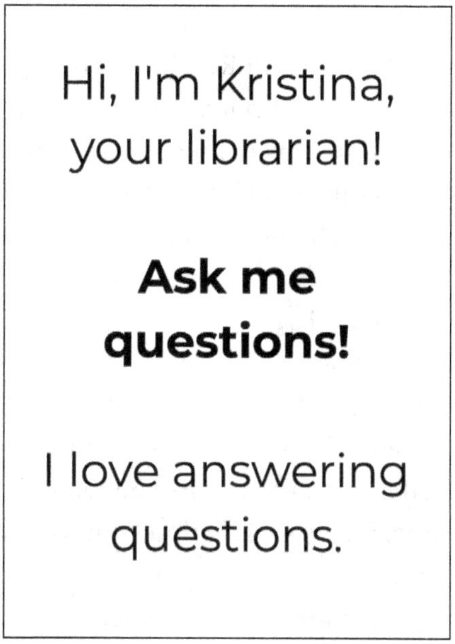

FIGURE 7.3
Image of a simple sign that was displayed each time the student success librarian visited Tobin House

Additional Resources

The student success librarian also created a LibGuide specifically for first-generation students[11] that was based on examples from other institutions. The guide has a landing page that supplies basic information about library services, including a welcome, the location of the library, and a description of what first-generation students are. The guide was created with first-generation students in mind, but can be used by all types of students. The rest of the guide includes a page on library lingo, basic library services, popular library spaces, finding books by call number, and an advertisement for the Tobin House Librarian-in-Residence program. The LibGuide is also linked on the Tobin House web page. The guide has received nearly 500 unique visits since September 2019, with most visitors using the Library Lingo page.

Outcomes

The Librarian-in-Residence program at Tobin House began on September 5, 2019, and continued until early March 2020, when the COVID-19 pandemic forced all university services and classes into online modes. During that six-month period, the student success librarian had twenty-two reference or research interactions with students. This was nearly twice the number of regular research or reference consultations that the student success librarian would have each semester. There were several other interactions with students when she helped them with information technology issues, such as setting up Microsoft Office applications (Outlook, Word, Excel, etc.) on their personal laptops. Many students had never had a personal laptop before and had only had access to computers at their high school, or they'd had laptops provided by their high school with all the necessary programs and software already installed. One student in particular met with the student success librarian three separate times to learn how to install Microsoft Office applications on her personal laptop, as she had never had to do that before. The librarian tried to refer the student to the university IT office, but after the second meeting it was clear that the student was far more comfortable interacting with the librarian than with IT—partly because of the convenience of having an information expert right in her dorm, and partly because she admitted it was overwhelming trying to figure out where to go for different technological solutions. This particular student became a frequent visitor to the Librarian-in-Residence hours and regularly sought out the student success librarian for assistance with her assignments.

Interactions like this made it abundantly clear that first-generation students, especially those coming from rural communities, were struggling with the sudden overwhelming privilege of having access to information as university students. Additionally, there were countless interactions with students who just wanted to chat and get to know their librarian. The overall sentiment was that Tobin House residents loved having a librarian on-site a couple days a week and that it made them feel more included in the academic community on campus. One overheard conversation consisted of a Tobin House resident telling their guest—quite emphatically—that the person sitting at the common table over there was their librarian, who was in the house a couple of days a week to help with assignments and "stuff."

It became much more difficult to connect with Tobin House residents during the COVID-19 pandemic, as all university residence halls were closed for many months. However, the residence coordinator sent out semi-regular e-mail communications to Tobin House residents reminding them about the virtual library services, resources, and experts still available to them. A few students reached out to say hello, but none of them requested research assistance during the COVID-19 pandemic. Because of the personal and in-person nature of the Librarian-in-Residence program at Tobin House, the program was essentially put on hold.

There is much more to be done at the University of Wyoming—and in the University of Wyoming Libraries—to help first-generation students adjust to the high level of information privilege that they experience upon enrollment, both in face-to-face and virtual learning environments. We plan to continue the Librarian-in-Residence program at Tobin House as soon as university regulations permit, to help first-generation students navigate the access to information that they receive as University of Wyoming students. There has also been an increased interest from other UW librarians in providing specialized outreach and engagement activities for first-generation students. Though the time that the student success librarian spent with Tobin House residents was short, it has great potential to be an effective, inclusive, and long-lasting outreach program that will grow deep and meaningful relationships between librarians and first-generation students at the University of Wyoming.

NOTES

1. Char Booth, "On Information Privilege," *Info-Mational* (blog). December 1, 2014, https://infomational.com/2014/12/01/on-information-privilege.
2. Charissa Powell, "Information Privilege and First-Year Students: A Case Study from a First-Year Seminar Course Using Access to Information as a Lens for Exploring Privilege," *In the Library with the Lead Pipe*, January 2020, www.inthelibrarywiththeleadpipe.org/2020/information-privilege; Heidi R. Johnson and Anna C. Smedly-Lopez, "Information Privilege in the Context of Community Engagement in Sociology," in *Disciplinary Applications of Information Literacy Threshold Concepts* (Chicago: Association of College & Research Libraries, 2017), 123–34; Sarah Hare and Cara Evanson, "Information Privilege Outreach for Undergraduate Students," *College & Research Libraries* 79, no. 6 (2018): 726–36, https://doi.org/10.5860/crl.79.6.726.

3. Nancy J. Becker, "Information Access," Computer Sciences, Encyclopedia.com, www.encyclopedia.com/computing/news-wires-white-papers-and-books/information-access.
4. Elise Schmelzer and Christine Peterson, "In Wyoming, Access to High-Speed Internet Depends on Where You Live," *Casper Star-Tribune Online*, 2018, https://trib.com/news/state-and-regional/in-wyoming-access-to-high-speed-internet-depends-on-where-you-live/article_1fb35fbb-de1d-5a89-b70b-fe4a2c9322cb.html.
5. Schmelzer and Peterson, "In Wyoming."
6. "UW First Generation Students," University of Wyoming, www.uwyo.edu/firstgeneration.
7. Peggy McIntosh, "White Privilege: Unpacking the Invisible Knapsack," National Seed Project, 1989, https://nationalseedproject.org/Key-SEED-Texts/white-privilege-unpacking-the-invisible-knapsack.
8. Xan Arch and Isaac Gilman, "First Principles: Designing Services for First-Generation Students," *College & Research Libraries* 80, no. 7 (2019): 996–1012, https://doi.org/10.5860/crl.80.7.996; Josefine Smith and Stacy Brinkman, "Information-Seeking Anxiety and Preferred Information Sources of First-Generation College Students," *Evidence Based Library and Information Practice* 16, no. 1 (2021): 5–24, https://doi.org/10.18438/eblip29843; Stephanie Graves, Sarah LeMire, and Kathy Christie Anders, "Uncovering the Information Literacy Skills of First-Generation and Provisionally Admitted Students," *Journal of Academic Librarianship* 47, no. 1 (2021): 102260, https://doi.org/10.1016/j.acalib.2020.102260.
9. Arch and Gilman, "First Principles."
10. "Welcome, First Generation Students!" University of Wyoming, www.uwyo.edu/firstgeneration.
11. Kristina Clement, "Library Resources for First Generation Students," University of Wyoming, https://uwyo.libguides.com/firstgeneration.

KARINA KLETSCHER AND JENNIFER TIRRELL

Aflame and Unafraid
A Case Study on Creating Interactive Programming in Remote Learning

In this case study we describe the creation, implementation, and outcome of an interactive and reflective series of virtual programs based in both the academic library and the Writing Center. We believe that discussions about social justice, the arts, and global citizenship belong in academic library programming because they are inherently valuable, are part of developing literacies, and are critical to fostering community and safe spaces for students who are spread out across the globe amidst immense external pressures. We share lessons learned from the series and how we can use these ideas, event formats, and digital tools to create an inclusive events program moving forward through and after the pandemic.

Our Institution

Soka University of America (SUA) is a private, nonprofit, four-year liberal arts college and graduate school in southern California. The total student body is around 400, 48 percent of whom are international students from 35 countries across the world. When COVID-19 struck, SUA closed its campus in March 2020 and all the students returned to their home states or countries to continue learning remotely. SUA, while nonsectarian, was founded on the Buddhist principles of peace, human rights, and the sanctity of life. The Daisaku and Kaneko Ikeda Library works to support students, faculty, and staff in meeting their academic and personal needs by providing access to information, teaching information literacy skills, and offering opportunities for the community to collaborate and engage in events that present various social and cultural topics and perspectives.

Background and Context

While the library has a history of building a collection and offering programming that reflects the community and its needs, when students and affinity groups planned and presented conferences and teach-ins in 2019, this sparked an even greater desire to ensure that underrepresented student groups felt they were represented in the library. Some new initiatives include purchasing library materials and creating online resources guides that reflect the student groups' input, and starting a social justice-oriented book club that meets bimonthly.

When planning the spring 2021 semester, we wanted to include an event around Amanda Gorman and her inaugural poem "The Hill We Climb" for poetry month in April. In the meantime, a colleague from the Writing Center reached out and asked about collaborating on an event on the same topic. She had worked with library staff a few years earlier on a successful Tupac poetry event and wanted to create a similar program. We felt that the recent impact of the presidential inauguration was a great opportunity to seize the moment and tie it to current social justice issues. Though our first event would take place in February, we were looking to transcend the boundaries of celebrating Black history or poetry in a given month by creating a series and an arts project that would span the spring semester. On another level, this vision included an interactive exhibition[1] that could be explored from anywhere in the world and could break down the isolating time zone and geographic boundaries that remote learning and work created. We wanted a personal and inclusive program that would give our community the opportunity to gather and engage in meaningful dialogue about the messages and social issues in Gorman's poem, how they reflect our students' concerns about our community, and the ways that students can be proactive global citizens in these turbulent times.

The Planning Committee

The Planning Committee for the event series grew organically from the relationship between the Ikeda Library and the Writing Center. There were four of us on the committee: two librarians and two writing specialists. Our respective roles and experience at SUA complemented each other well. SUA writing specialists are part-time staff with a set number of hours per semester as compared to the librarians, who are traditional full-time staff. While both librarians had been in their roles at SUA for two years or less, the writing specialists had been at the university for many years and had held additional roles as instructors of record, which lent institutional experience and deeper connections with faculty. This meant that our committee could remain small and then liaise to our various campus connections, such as the performing and visual arts faculty and SUA's newest unit: the Office of Diversity, Equity, and Inclusion. Each of us was able to use our unique strengths and experience to contribute, from design to events and cultural programming. But most importantly, we all had experience in working with students in a one-on-one capacity, as well as empathy and an ethics of care for the students and the broader campus community.

The Process

Starting in January 2021, the committee met to brainstorm ideas for the events, decide on their content and format, identify tasks, delegate responsibilities, establish deadlines, and create materials. We met on a regular basis via MS Teams video and communicated through MS Teams chat and e-mail. We also created a shared folder in Box, our campus cloud management tool, so that we could easily upload, access, and edit all materials related to the events.

The event series was another opportunity to engage students with the library and its resources. We created a LibGuide[2] in order to have a centralized location for all event information, resources on Amanda Gorman, and library catalog links to collections from poets that Gorman admires. We hoped that funneling all attendee traffic through the LibGuide during each event would serve as a reminder that the library's collections were still accessible to our global community for both academic and leisure purposes.

Building on trends such as virtual reality (VR) and creative place-making, the committee wanted to go beyond a static website gallery for the art exhibition to create an immersive gathering space. However, without VR equipment or a budget, we researched open access or freemium platforms that did not require coding experience or special gear. We ultimately decided on ArtSteps, "a web-based environment" specifically designed to host "virtual art galleries in lifelike 3D spaces."[3] We loved the fact that this platform supported many art mediums, had simple design functions, included ready-made templates, and could be accessed over the internet. Due to time constraints, we opted for a pre-designed gallery space, which took one person approximately sixteen hours to set up. ArtSteps mainly requires time and patience to upload, place, and scale each artwork and its description. Graphics other than student artwork, like murals and virtual signage, were created in Canva and then uploaded to the platform. We had planned to stream Gorman's inaugural delivery in the space, but the video feature was dysfunctional, so we opted for a static image instead.

The Aflame and Unafraid Series

The program was a two-part event series titled "Aflame and Unafraid," taken from a line of Amanda Gorman's "The Hill We Climb." We had initially envisioned a three-part series that would connect with various celebrations

FIGURE 8.1
Interior view of one of the exhibition galleries

FIGURE 8.2
Aerial view of the exhibition

such as Black History Month and National Poetry Month, as well as move beyond those specific activities to demonstrate that topics of social justice are essential ongoing conversations rather than only being tied to specific themes and months. We wanted the series to support informal learning opportunities that would enable our widespread community to gather and engage in creative and reflective ways. However, in view of the broader university calendar of events taking place, we decided to hold two events, one in February and one in April. Additionally, by not holding the second event in March, the community had time to reflect on what had been presented and discussed in the first event and then create their artistic response to be displayed at the second event.

In scheduling the days and times for each event, we considered that our international community is currently spread across multiple time zones and the class schedule format of Mondays/Wednesdays/Fridays and Tuesdays/Thursdays. We chose to hold the events at 11:30 a.m. and 5:15 p.m. Pacific Standard Time for one hour each, since both these times coincided with the standardized mealtimes at SUA and are thus free from scheduled classes. Also, the morning time slot best accommodated European and the Americas time zones, while the evening time slot best accommodated Asian time zones. We staggered the Community Dialogues events on Tuesday and Wednesday and the Opening Party events on Thursday and Friday so that the same course structures were not negatively impacted.

We advertised both events via the library's and the Writing Center's social media platforms, community e-mails, the SUA online calendar, and the community-wide "SUA Today" newsletter.

Community Dialogues Event

The Community Dialogues took place via Zoom on February 23 at 11:30 a.m. with 24 people attending and on February 24 at 5:15 p.m. with 20 people attending. The dialogues were designed as a social opportunity for people to interact, share, and learn from each other. We discussed the different themes from Gorman's poem and how they represented and connected to the racial injustice and violence incidents nationwide. We also hoped that this event in particular would reach out to those students and community

FIGURE 8.3
Marketing for the Community Dialogues, Virtual Exhibition, and the Opening Party

members who were experiencing social and racial injustice firsthand, along with those who were anxious or angry about these incidents; and the event would provide a safe and supportive space in which to be heard.

We prepared a short PowerPoint that included introductory remarks which explained our motivation and the purpose of the event; a video of

Gorman's inaugural poem;[4] and guiding questions in case of conversational lulls, such as "Do you hear/see yourself represented anywhere in the lines of this poem? If so, where?" and "How has this poem impacted your understanding of social justice and racial inequity?" And finally, we included a link to the event's LibGuide, which provided related resources in order to contextualize the moment and poem in sociocultural and historical frames. After playing the video, we shared the questions in chat and moved into breakout rooms for discussion before regrouping to share takeaways.

Virtual Exhibition and the Opening Party

The second event in our series was an Opening Party to celebrate the launch of the virtual exhibition of submitted artworks on the online platform, ArtSteps. These events took place on April 8 at 11:30 a.m. with 15 attendees and on April 9 at 5:15 p.m. with 11 attendees. Throughout the month of March, we had standing calls for artwork and were collecting the responses through a Qualtrics registration form.

Exhibition submissions were open to the entire SUA community and could be in any artistic medium, including poetry, studio art, multimedia, and audio. We wanted to allow as many of our community members as possible to participate in whatever medium they felt most comfortable with. We required participants to write a gallery label description of 50–75 words (guidelines and examples were provided in our LibGuide) and agree to a short Artwork and Publicity Release Statement, as the exhibition would be public. Additionally, attendance at the Opening Party was not dependent on submitting artwork. We received a total of thirteen art submissions, all from students, which ranged from digital paintings to embroidery to a poetry recording.

As with the Community Dialogues, we began with short introductory remarks on the "Aflame and Unafraid" series, then showed Gorman's inaugural delivery of "The Hill We Climb." The original ArtSteps exhibition was unable to be completed in time for the Opening Party dates. Instead, a committee member presented the artworks and artist descriptions in a slide deck, and as a group we viewed and conversed about each piece, in a manner similar to an intimate docent tour.

Assessment

We gathered informal and formal feedback from attendees so that we could assess the impact of both events and use the information to help us plan for future events. During the events, people shared their responses in chat and at the closing portion of the events. After each event, we sent out a survey to get further feedback in an anonymous format.

Attendees shared that the Community Dialogues spoke to them in different ways. Some specific thoughts expressed were "the need to speak the truth," "being open to listening to others," "engaging in personal growth," and "raising awareness of and doing more to address injustices." One student connected Gorman's themes to a viral video by Cuban artists that called for unity to address Cuba's oppression and social injustice. Another student connected Gorman's poetry to a well-known Korean poet, which ultimately inspired her to write a poem for the exhibition. With regard to the Virtual Exhibition, several people thanked us for providing the space to display and view student art: "I'm so grateful for this space you have created for artists to share their work." Some of the artists expressed their gratitude for the opportunity to create and show their art, as well as for the positive feedback they received about their pieces.

With the two surveys, we only received eight responses, but it was still valuable information. People appreciated the opportunity during the Community Dialogues to share with and listen to each other in an "authentic manner" about "important issues." Some suggestions were to make the events longer and to offer similar opportunities to "connect and learn together" in the future. One respondent to the Virtual Exhibition survey commented: "the event provided another opportunity for me to recommit myself to the work of creating a just, peaceful society for all."

We were delighted to learn that, overall, these were successful events. While we would have loved a larger gathering, we appreciate that the impact was the greater value, and we are thrilled that people were comfortable and happy with their experience.

Challenges

We faced three main challenges throughout the process of coordinating the series and designing the exhibition. The first challenge was promoting the series and attracting participants for both the events and the exhibition. Despite leveraging our campus connections and available promotional outlets, most of our participants belonged to one course led by a faculty member with whom the committee had strong ties. However, the challenges of campus community outreach during remote learning have not been unique to this event and require reflection at the overall library level.

A second challenge was the unanticipated limitations of virtual programming. Initially, our idea was to host a virtual gallery reception, encouraging attendees to dress up—if desired—and allowing free exploration of the exhibition during a short program of remarks or performances from participating artists. We soon realized that our vision was a bit more than we could orchestrate, as the casual organic flow and interaction of a real-time gallery opening was not truly reproducible in an online format. We were also a bit concerned about attendance due to general Zoom fatigue and the low turnout at our first event, so we decided to reformat the opening as a docent tour.

The third challenge was due to one committee member's conflicting professional and personal schedules, which severely limited their ability to contribute. This led to the exhibition being incomplete at the time of our Virtual Exhibition dates, though we were able to reassign roles to present the works in other ways at the event and complete the exhibition later. The timeline pushback also meant that we were still tweaking the accessibility features in ArtSteps long after the series ended and the exhibition was published. Two adjustments were adding pop-up text for screen-readers throughout the virtual space and an automatic guided tour option. However, the latter update is partially unreliable on different devices. To combat ArtSteps's obstacles in visibility, navigation controls, broadband strength, and the possible motion sickness that people may experience in immersive virtual environments, we redesigned our static slide presentation of the artworks to be perpetually available on the guide. Reframing these challenges as solution and learning opportunities has given us a framework for improving our collaboration and programming in the future.

Future Considerations

The event series has been a great exercise in rethinking access at future programming. Online platforms like Zoom and ArtSteps helped us to maintain a broad audience across time and geography. They also gave students choices in participation modes, as they had the freedom not only to speak, type, or simply listen, but also to create art or just have a place to gather and view the art. We plan on including streaming components and other creative digital tools at future in-person events in order to sustain this ease of access and flexibility with student schedules and personal needs, while still maintaining the organic feel and flow unique to in-person gatherings.

Another consideration is bringing student groups into planning committees to cohost programs. We want to offer students the opportunity to design and lead discussions. We would greatly benefit from their perspectives, as well as utilize their social capital in order to build attendance. It is difficult to know precisely what contributed to the low turnouts at the events; potential factors include Zoom fatigue, schedules, a competing event calendar, marketing efforts, and both librarians being fairly new and therefore not having established campus connections and relationships. Having greater student connections and expertise would give us better insight into these factors and possible solutions.

Conclusion

The "Aflame and Unafraid" series has given us a renewed sense of how an academic library can contribute to an inclusive campus climate. By designing a scaffolded programming series that provides safe spaces to reflect, discuss, create, and ultimately connect, we are fostering our community's relationships and cultural competencies. These are spaces and opportunities that students may not typically have amidst the immense external pressures that social issues impose on their academic and personal lives. We have felt this as staff, and greatly enjoyed the bonds created over our collective vulnerability during these events; moreover, these bonds have continued afterwards as we have met for consultations with several student attendees who may never have reached out to the library before the series. By rethinking and leveraging the library's role as well as mixing event formats and new tools, all amplified by collaborations with more campus entities (and especially students), we hope that this is just the beginning in building a more inclusive outreach program that will support student comfortability and growth.

NOTES

1. "Aflame & Unafraid: A Virtual Exhibition," ArtSteps, https://bit.ly/AflameAndUnafraid.
2. "Aflame and Unafraid: Events & Exhibition Guide: The Virtual Exhibition," Daisaku and Kaneko Ikeda Library: Soka University of America, LibGuide, http://bit.ly/AflameAndAfraid_Guide.
3. ArtSteps, www.artsteps.com.
4. "Amanda Gorman Reads Inauguration Poem, 'The Hill We Climb,'" YouTube video, 5:52, posted by *PBS NewsHour*, January 20, 2021, www.youtube.com/watch?v=LZ055ilIiN4.

TARIANA SMITH

9

Inclusive Programming
Empathy, Support, and Access as Foundational Tools

In a rapidly changing learning and social environment, academic libraries have a responsibility to students to provide inclusive programming to meet to their diverse needs. Academic libraries should strive to be multicultural and multifaceted in creating accessible programming for all types of students. Considering students' contexts and lived experiences enhances collaboration efforts, diversity, and relationships among students and the surrounding community. Meeting students within their contexts creates opportunities for empowered learning, fosters dialogue on social and political issues, and helps build relationships and community partnerships.[1] Academic libraries should not only house the resources that students use, but be resources in themselves to address student needs and concerns. Fostering empathy, giving support, and providing access are all foundational tools that academic libraries should consider when implementing inclusive programming and creating an inclusive culture.

Empathy

Empathy is the act of understanding, being aware of, being sensitive to, or vicariously experiencing the feelings, thoughts, and experiences of others. Understanding is something all students need, and it serves as an integral part of empathy. When developing inclusive programming, understanding the needs of individual students, rather than as a collective, helps us build relationships with students so that they see themselves within the library. Awareness is another essential aspect of empathy. Librarians can become aware of student needs by having conversations and dialogue that connect them with students and build personal relationships. Librarians must understand that discussing complex issues concerning students and worldly matters may be difficult. However, understanding each student's lived experience and how it impacts their learning environment can provide insight for academic libraries to implement the best strategies with which to support students' needs.

Supporting Diverse Students

When considering the context of the students, diversity is a primary factor. Students come with different lived experiences that have shaped their worldviews, motivations, and their ability and readiness to learn. Diversity concerns, but is not limited to, gender, race, ethnicity, age, sexual orientation, culture, disabilities or exceptionalities, gender identity, socioeconomic status, religious beliefs, employment status, and more. The Louisiana State University Libraries invited the vice provost for diversity and chief diversity officer to conduct a workshop on diversity for library staff, entitled Diversity 101.[2] Developing partnerships on campus with other entities and organizations fosters collaboration, and diversity training can help equip librarians with the empathy and understanding needed to serve students from diverse populations. The University of Denver Libraries creates booklists for students to explore several topics and issues and provides research guides to support their campus courses related to multicultural issues.[3] These research guides provide insight on anti-racism, Asian studies, gender and women studies, religious studies, and more. These academic libraries have made their stance known in supporting diverse and inclusive efforts for students. Adopting methodologies centered on critical multiculturalism, cultural capital, and critical pedagogy will ensure that students from all backgrounds, primarily marginalized or vulnerable groups, receive the equitable resources, services, and support they need.

Cultural Capital, Multiculturalism, and Critical Pedagogy

Acknowledging and understanding that each student comes with cultural capital—a vibrant series of life experiences that shape their mindset, perceptions, perspective, and worldview—will aid inclusive programming within academic libraries. Students come to educational settings with a wealth of knowledge from all walks of life, and every experience and encounter that a student brings with them to an educational setting is valuable and enriching. These experiences help librarians learn more about the students and how to engage them, and integrating this knowledge into academic library programming establishes a foundation of empathy and understanding, which ultimately serve as foundational tools for inclusive programming. When developing inclusive programs within the academic library, librarians should use these experiences to embed students' cultural capital within the programming.

The diverse and multicultural backgrounds that students come from should be used to illuminate inclusive programming. Academic libraries should serve as resources and tools for students to discuss, learn about, and investigate various multicultural issues worldwide. Diversity and inclusion directly correlate with one another and involve acknowledging the different backgrounds of students. Academic libraries should bring these social issues to the forefront in order to create a space and environment for students to engage in transformative discussion. Creating inclusive programming using a multicultural education approach can address bias, prejudice, discrimination, misconceptions, and worldviews. For example, the University of North Carolina at Chapel Hill established the Reckoning Initiative in fall 2019 after the George Floyd killing: this shared learning initiative in the College of Arts and Sciences was designed to address and foster dialogue on complex topics concerning race, heritage, politics, post-conflict legacies, and more.[4] The initiative incorporated two courses, shared readings, and forums to discuss these issues while also engaging the wider community. Initiatives like this one provide opportunities for students to learn from one another and discuss critical worldly problems that affect their everyday lives. Libraries can similarly foster inclusion and reach students from diverse backgrounds by developing inclusive programming through critical pedagogy.

As an academic unit, the academic library is responsible for empowering students through resources, services, and programming that reflect their needs. Academic librarians should ask themselves why inclusive programming is essential and examine what they are doing, not only as a collective but as individuals, to live, breathe, and implement these foundational tools that can help support students' needs. Critical pedagogy can help inform programming by making it more equitable through developing critical thinking skills, challenging societal norms, and giving students the space and autonomy to inquire about worldly issues. When considering cultural capital and multiculturalism, critical pedagogy helps foster dialogue concerning the issues. Providing this support helps create a sense of relatedness and belonging within the library.

Relatedness and Belonging

Creating a space and place of belonging and relatedness is an integral component of inclusive programming for students, specifically vulnerable groups. Many students within vulnerable groups already come to college with an increased load, responsibilities, obligations, and life experiences. Academic libraries must meet students where they are and provide the support necessary for students to feel that they belong in the academic environment. Doing this means ensuring that personal relationships are built with students to show understanding, support, and empathy for them. Ormrod argues that establishing relatedness and belonging environments will help students be more intrinsically motivated.[5] Although intrinsic motivation does not ultimately rely on outside factors, creating environments rooted in relatedness and belonging can help students feel connected not only to their environment but to their selves as well, by helping to build their self-confidence. Inclusive programming involves creating environments where students feel like they belong and can relate to their context and peers. Student-centered programming uses student-rich experiences to provide a supportive learning environment while engaging them through relatedness and belonging. One example of inclusive programming was undertaken by Southern University at New Orleans' Leonard S. Washington Memorial Library, which hosted Instagram "Talk Back Sessions" during the early stages of the COVID-19 pandemic. Librarians held Instagram sessions three or four times a week, providing a platform for students to share their concerns and express their feelings about life during the pandemic, while librarians discussed the library's resources and services and identified outside resources for assistance.[6] As a result, the students were appreciative and felt they had support from the library during a difficult time. Creating a social climate of relatedness also supports students in that students can relate to one another and their circumstances.

Support

Support involves providing resources and services, of course, but it also has an emotional and social aspect. Students from vulnerable groups face many barriers and challenges stemming from economic, social, political, and educational situations, and education is something that should be afforded to and equitable for every student. Students need supportive environments to alleviate their loads in life, in order to ensure student access and success. Providing resources and services for students demonstrates empathy and creates a supportive space for students to build self-efficacy. Supporting students means building relationships with them in order to identify the barriers and challenges they face. However, it is not enough to identify the obstacles. Those barriers need to be removed for students to feel secure and confident within themselves and the learning environment. Even in the most challenging situations, when students feel they have support and the tools they need to overcome those challenges, they are more likely to push forward.

Identifying Barriers

Meeting students within their context creates the opportunity for empowered learning, autonomy, and collaboration between academic libraries and students in a rapidly changing learning environment. Building relationships with students is an essential aspect of connecting with them and embracing their lived experiences. McClusky's "theory of margin" encourages educators to consider each student's power-load margin (PLM). "Margin is a function of the relationship of load to power. By load we mean the self and social demands required by a person to maintain a minimal level of autonomy. By power we mean the resources, i.e., abilities, possessions, position, allies, etc., which a person can command in coping with load."[7] Sometimes barriers involve a lack of understanding of library terminology, a poor grasp of information literacy, or even having issues using technology.[8] Identifying students' emotional and social needs enhances their feeling of relatedness and belonging within the library. Collaborating with students to identify their barriers will help build personal relationships and inclusive practices, while also providing insight into the best practices, methods, and strategies to use in inclusive library programming that can eliminate those barriers.

Removing Barriers

Students experience multiple barriers throughout their academic careers, and collaborating with students to identify their barriers will catalyze determining how to remove or mitigate those barriers. Students can articulate the issues and the types of services that are needed to help them overcome their obstacles. Obstacles involving time, parental obligations, jobs, health, and other issues are all barriers that students face daily. Gold (2005) emphasizes the importance of creating comfortable environments, creating meaningful instruction, promoting active learning, and increasing flexibility and immersion throughout the learning experience.[9]

The University Libraries at the University of North Carolina at Chapel Hill (UNC) have an Inclusion, Diversity, Equity, and Accessibility (IDEA) Council. This council is comprised of individuals from diverse backgrounds, and is focused on creating and building an inclusive environment for both library employees and library users. IDEA serves to foster inclusion and equity. Establishing a council such as this could help create a dialogue between librarians and students while providing a platform to implement change and remove barriers for students. The council provides and develops numerous resources on implicit bias, desegregation of the university, immigration, student protest, LGBTQ, and more.[10] The University Libraries also have an "inclusive excellence librarian" who sits on the leadership team and focuses on advancing diversity efforts.[11] Removing barriers and giving students the resources, tools, and platform to address their needs will also help build their self-efficacy. Self-efficacy is the ability or capability that students have to accomplish tasks.[12] Students must believe in themselves and have confidence in themselves in order to complete tasks and achieve in life. Building this inner confidence leads to intrinsically motivated and self-regulated students[13] while increasing students' ability to confidently access resources.

Access

Access is another aspect of serving marginalized groups, and involves providing multiple channels for students to access information while considering the context of each student.[14] Each student's load varies and impacts their drive and ability to remain motivated within the learning environment. Academic libraries serve as gateways to advance the quality of learning, foster inclusion, and drive down education costs by implementing support strategies for students, providing multiple access points for resources and services, and creating empathetic environments for students to express their lived experiences. These types of strategies offer insight on effective methods that academic libraries should implement to empower students and build self-efficacy in their learning environments, no matter what their background or circumstances are.

An example of this type of gateway is the Affordable Learning LOUISiana Initiative. The Louisiana Library Network, through the initiative, partners with libraries and faculty to increase access to instructional materials through the use of affordable educational resources (AER), open educational resources (OER), and open access content.[15] Doing this ensures that students from all backgrounds, including those from vulnerable and marginalized groups, have the same access to resources as their peers. AER, OER, and open access content decrease the load of the student and increase their power. As a result, students feel more confident in completing their assignments while feeling supported within their educational environment.

Exceptionality (Disability) Services

Some students need extra attention or accommodations to ensure that they have access to library resources, services, and programming. These students' exceptionalities can be accommodated by academic libraries that are innovative, strategic, empathetic, and inclusive. Exceptionalities are not challenges, but rather opportunities for academic libraries to grow and engage more with students from all backgrounds. Through the College of Communication and Information, Florida State University's Project PALS is a series of self-paced instructional modules for librarians and library staff to learn more about people living with autism.[16] This series of modules, created by librarians and experts in the autism field, provides insight into persons living on the autism spectrum. The modules are designed to educate and equip librarians and staff with the knowledge and tools they need to interact and work with individuals on the autism spectrum.

Working with students to develop inclusive programming would acknowledge their cultural capital and multiculturalism, while also enhancing their self-efficacy and critical thinking skills. Ensuring that adequate and proper technology is used throughout the library's programming will help reach a broader audience, while also giving the target audience access to content and information. An example of this approach is the Adaptive Technology Center at Southeastern University in Hammond, Louisiana, which is equipped with software and technology to provide access for students with exceptionalities. The lab computer has features and software such as a large-print keyboard, PowerVision magnifying reader, Adobe Acrobat Reader, Roxio Creator, Nuance Dragon Naturally Speaking, and much more.[17] Syracuse University's Project ENABLE (Expanding Non-Discriminatory Access by Librarians Everywhere)[18] is a free professional development program that provides training to "library professionals from all types of libraries in order to build their capacity for providing equitable access and services to students with disabilities, an underserved population."[19]

Conclusion

Inclusive programming is collaborative, multicultural, supportive, accessible, and empathetic. Academic libraries can serve as the bridge to resources, tools, and platforms that can support students from all backgrounds and give students a sense of belonging and relatedness in their academic libraries. Inclusive programming begins with empathy and building relationships with our students. Understanding where students come from and the life obligations they face will establish relatability and provide insight into how academic librarians can better serve students. Providing support to students by alleviating their loads will increase their power and help build self-efficacy by giving them the tools and resources they need to succeed. Implementing inclusive strategies and practices is not just an action but a culture. Libraries must create professional development opportunities for library faculty and staff concerning sensitivity and empathy, disabilities, multiculturalism, access, and support. Ensuring that library programming is accessible fosters inclusion and supports diverse learners. Empathy, support, and access are three critical foundational tools for developing inclusive academic library programming. As academic librarians, we must remember our role as a resource and our responsibility to create an inclusive environment and programming that students can relate to and see their existence reflected in.

NOTES

1. Philip C. Candy, *Self-Direction for Lifelong Learning: A Comprehensive Guide to Theory and Practice* (San Francisco: Jossey-Bass, 1991).
2. "Employees of the Libraries Attend Diversity 101 Workshop," Louisiana State University Libraries, February 4, 2020, http://news.blogs.lib.lsu.edu/2020/02/06/employees-of-the-libraries-attend-diversity-101-workshop.
3. "University Libraries: Inclusive Excellence at the University Libraries," University of Denver University Libraries, n.d., https://library.du.edu/inclusive-excellence.html.
4. "Reckoning: Race, Memory, and Reimagining the Public University: A Shared Learning Initiative for Fall 2019," UNC College of Arts and Sciences, 2019, https://reckoning.unc.edu.
5. Jeanne Ellis Ormrod, *Human Learning*, 8th ed. (Hoboken, NJ: Pearson, 2020).
6. SUNO Library (sunolibrary), "Adjusting to a New Normal Can Be Overwhelming. We Want to Open Up a Space to Hear Your Challenges," Instagram, March 31, 2020, www.instagram.com/p/B-aYyC-J43k/?igshid=4vfnoyz00riw.
7. H. Y. McClusky, "A Dynamic Approach to Participation in Community Development," *Journal of Community Development Society* 1, no. 1 (1970), 25–32, https://doi.org/10.1080/15575330.1970.10877417.
8. D. P. Teague, "Tips for Teaching Library Instruction and Information Literacy to First-Gen College Students, Nontraditional Students, or English as a Second Language (ESL) Students," *Serials Review* 45, no. 3, 105–10, https://doi-org.ezproxy.baylor.edu/10.1080/00987913.2019.1644699.
9. H. E. Gold, "Engaging the Adult Learner: Creating Effective Library Instruction," *Libraries and the Academy* 5, no. 4 (2005), 467–81, https://doi.org/10.1353/pla.2005.0051.
10. "Inclusion, Diversity, Equity, and Accessibility (IDEA)," University of North Carolina at Chapel Hill Libraries, n.d., https://library.unc.edu/IDEA.

11. Adrianne Gibilisco, "Diversity Spotlight: Elaine Westbrooks," UNC Office of the Provost for Diversity and Inclusion, July 31, 2020, https://diversity.unc.edu/2020/07/diversity-spotlight-elaine-westbrooks.
12. A. Bandura, "Self-Efficacy: Toward a Unifying Theory of Behavioral Change," *Psychological Review* 84 (1977): 191–215.
13. V. R. Lukić, M. Marić, and S. Štrangarić, "Relational Impact of Cultural Capital and the Perception of Self-Efficacy on Educational Achievement," *TEME: Casopis Za Društvene Nauke* 44, no. 4 (2020): 1261–74, https://doi.org/10.22190/TEME190321077R.
14. Candy, *Self-Direction for Lifelong Learning*, 1991.
15. "Choice. Affordability. Accessibility," Louisiana Library Network LOUIS, https://louislibraries.org/alearningla.
16. "About PALS," Project PALS College of Communication & Information, Florida State University, n.d., https://pals.cci.fsu.edu.
17. "For Library Users with Disabilities," Sims Memorial Library, Southeastern Louisiana University, n.d., https://selu.libguides.com/c.php?g=690371&p=4881691.
18. Project Enable, "Our History," Syracuse University, https://projectenable.syr.edu/OurHistory.
19. Project ENABLE, "About Us," Syracuse University, https://projectenable.syr.edu/AboutUs.

JASON COLEMAN, LIS PANKL, AND LEO S. LO

10

Student Well-Being and Libraries

Addressing Systemic Racism and COVID-19

Throughout the history of higher education, student success has required much more than educators with the knowledge and skill to facilitate learning. A student who lacks food, has mental health challenges, endures threats and assaults, or lacks social support is likely to underperform, and cannot flourish. While these basic human needs have always been present, many of those who interact with today's students claim that these needs have grown more pronounced over the past decade or even longer. The literature of higher education is now filled with reports of students' declining mental health, loneliness, lack of a feeling of belonging, financial distress, suicide, and drug use. While these challenges are present among all categories of students, they are particularly severe among BIPOC students and those with minoritized gender identities.[1]

Universities have begun to respond to these rapidly intensifying needs by creating institutional structures dedicated to addressing what is being widely referred to as the "well-being crisis."[2] Academic libraries have been joining, and in some cases leading, these institutional efforts. Collectively, their responses have involved changes to policies and practices in nearly every aspect of library operations. Numerous libraries have created wellness or well-being committees to create action plans and establish the libraries as a safe haven and space for connecting with others. In this chapter, we explore the concepts of well-being and wellness, examine the literature in order to see how minoritized students are differentially experiencing the well-being crisis, and describe several interventions that libraries are using in an attempt to address the crisis.

Student Well-Being and Wellness

There are no universally recognized definitions of *well-being* or *wellness* in the context of college students. Many descriptions of wellness invoke a medical model in which "unwellness" is viewed as a state in which there are deficits, and "wellness" is a state in which no deficits exist. Wellness is viewed as a state that can be defined and modeled. Well-being, by contrast, has no normative baseline and no upper or lower boundaries. It is a subjective state that resists attempts at concretization or dimensional reduction. But while well-being is nebulous, it is clear that it includes and goes beyond wellness. Rose Pascarell, vice-president for student life at George Mason University, offers a definition of well-being that illustrates its breadth and character. She defines it as "living a life of vitality, purpose, resilience, and engagement."[3]

There are multidimensional models of wellness. These dimensions are interconnected; deficits in one dimension may create deficits in others. The College of William & Mary has a website that lists eight dimensions of wellness: emotional, financial, environmental, intellectual, social, occupational, physical, and spiritual.[4] The website provides a separate page for each of these dimensions, each of which gives a definition, tips, and lists campus resources related to that dimension. The physical dimension refers to bodily health; the intellectual to having an orientation toward learning and sharing knowledge; the emotional to understanding and constructively responding to one's own feelings and those of others; the social to connecting positively to others; the spiritual to finding meaning and purpose; the vocational to doing work that is fulfilling; the financial to effectively managing resources; and the environmental refers to being aware of the ways in which the environment impacts us and we impact the environment.

The Well-Being Crisis among Minoritized Students

Prior to the global COVID-19 pandemic, the mental and emotional health of college students had already been in decline for several years.[5] The pandemic has made the situation much worse. The Fall 2020 Healthy Minds Study of nearly 33,000 college students found that 39 percent of them screened positive for clinical depression, 34 percent screened positive for anxiety disorders, 83 percent had mental or emotional difficulties that had hurt their academic performance in the past four weeks, and nearly two-thirds of them felt left out or isolated. Even more alarming, 23 percent had intentionally injured themselves in the past year and 13 percent had thought about suicide.[6]

When one focuses on students from vulnerable populations, the picture becomes even bleaker. Students of color and those experiencing poverty are more likely to face financial stress and are more likely to have experienced the death of a loved one during the pandemic.[7] A recent survey of nearly 50,000 students who were seeking treatment from a college counseling center examined how the pandemic had differentially impacted the mental health of students from vulnerable groups.[8] The pandemic's greatest negative impact on students' financial status, personal health, grief/loss, and food/housing insecurity was seen in those who identify as American Indian or Alaskan Native.[9] The impact of grief and loss on mental health was also much higher among those who identify as African American/Black and Native Hawaiian or Pacific Islander than among those who identify as white.[10] Students identifying as Asian American, African American/Black, or native Hawaiian or Pacific Islander reported that they had encountered the most discrimination or harassment.[11] The highest impact in almost every dimension examined was seen in students who identify as pansexual or queer.[12]

But the extent of the crisis among these populations cannot be explained by recent events alone. Discrimination, institutionalized disenfranchisement, and endemic racism had been undermining their well-being long before this past year. Crucially, research from the Wellbeing Collaborative shows that the greater the number of marginalized identities with which a student identifies, the less likely they are to report that they have a sense of well-being.[13] According to the JED Foundation, first-year African American college students are more likely than their white peers to report feeling overwhelmed most or all of the time during their first term.[14] And the results of a 2015 Harris poll showed that students of color are also less likely to seek help than their white peers.[15]

But there is reason to hope that these trends can be reversed. According to a survey of more than 400 college and university presidents conducted in

2019, 80 percent of them viewed mental health and well-being as a greater priority than it had been three years earlier.[16] A recent report from the Chronicle of Higher Education highlights how some colleges and universities have been radically reconceiving their institutional approach to well-being.[17] For example, George Mason University is focusing on equity and inclusive well-being.[18] And at nearby George Washington University, there is an increasing emphasis on defining well-being in terms of mattering.[19] In recognition of the need to respond meaningfully to the crisis, universities are beginning to establish high-level administrative positions dedicated to well-being.[20] Examples include titles such as Dean of Wellness, and Assistant Vice President for Health, Safety, and Well-being Initiatives.[21]

Academic Libraries Respond to the Well-Being Crisis

With their focus on equitable services to all and their intersections with the academic, research, and outreach missions of their parent institutions, academic libraries have unique opportunities to expand their role in supporting student well-being.[22] Prior to the unsettling events of 2020, academic libraries had been taking advantage of their boundary-spanning role to implement a variety of programs, new services, and changed practices that were intended to address the declining sense of well-being seen in college students.[23] Examples of these practices include selling sexual health products in vending machines, delivering library instruction to improve intellectual wellness, providing research guides related to wellness topics, hosting food pantries, partnering with other campus units to provide wellness tips, creating and furnishing comfortable spaces for napping or socializing, and providing meditation and prayer rooms.[24] The Association of College & Research Libraries recognized this groundswell of effort by including student well-being among its 2020 list of top trends in academic libraries.[25]

Many academic libraries have partnered with other campus offices and programs to gain needed expertise, access to additional methods to promote services, and expanded access to labor and funding. The University of California Berkeley Library system partnered with the university's student association, Health Services, and Wellness Fund to create napping areas in three libraries.[26] Albertson's Library at Boise State University has partnered with Health Services to provide healthy snacks, flu shots, and access to peer educators who give stress management tips and help students to find reliable health information.[27] Albertson's Library has also partnered with the Campus Assessment Resource and Education program to help students report behaviors that may indicate mental health issues and help them find assistance with mental health conditions.[28] California State University at Northridge's library partnered with Health Services to provide meditation sessions during finals week.[29] And the Kansas State University Libraries have partnered with Counseling Services for de-stressing events with animals and has partnered with Recreational Services to offer yoga sessions during finals week. Opportunities to bring campus services like these into the library should expand even more as universities adopt increasingly holistic approaches to student well-being. Teresa Helena Moreno and Jennifer M. Jackson, librarians at the University of Illinois at Chicago (UIC), redesigned an Undergraduate Engagement Program to focus on the needs of underrepresented and marginalized students.[30] Through this program, UIC librarians have assisted writing tutors from the Writing Center and have partnered with their campus cultural centers to offer a film series.[31]

Other libraries have primarily used internal resources to address well-being. In the spring of 2021, Penn State University created three "Wellness Days" in lieu of spring break due to the pandemic.[32] There were no classes on these Wellness Days, and each day focused on two dimensions of wellness. The University Libraries were one of the major contributors to the initiative; they provided a financial literacy guide to help students navigate the world of student loans and other forms of financial aid, provided a personal health and wellness guide, and "sponsored book clubs surrounding the themes of intellectual and spiritual wellness, as well as overcoming adversity."[33] The libraries also provided the chosen books to student organizations. Louisiana State University Libraries created a relaxation room to help students de-stress during finals week.[34] They outfitted the room with "a sensory table with calm-down bottles, aromatherapy with scented oil, kinetic sand, stress balls, word puzzles, and 'fun' furniture like inflatable chairs and bean bags."[35] North Carolina State University Libraries created a Twitch channel that allows patrons to watch others engage in calming activities like knitting, painting plants, or playing games.[36] Megan Otto, one of their digital media specialists, developed a sound bath meditation exercise. The University of California at San Diego Libraries have a "De-Stress Activities" page on the main navigation menu of their website. The page is filled with creative approaches to supporting student well-being both virtually and within the library itself. The approaches suggested include virtual study rooms, a virtual coloring club, a library de-stress publication, walkstations, foam rollers for stretching, DIY Zen gardens, and kinetic sand.[37]

These are just a small sampling of the many innovative approaches that academic libraries have implemented to improve student well-being. Information about the impact of these activities is scarce. However, as universities develop more concerted approaches to assessing student well-being and determining what does and does not help with student retention, we anticipate that evaluation will become the norm rather than the exception.

Lessons Learned

Student well-being is crucial to both student success and the long-term viability of higher education. As universities grapple with the simultaneous public health crises of COVID-19 and systemic racism, the ways that resources are allocated are changing at a rapid pace. For example, in the past six months there has been an explosion of high-level administrative jobs that focus on issues of diversity, equity, inclusion, and anti-racism (DEIA). And equally importantly, the recruitment and retention of BIPOC students is being given increasing weight. For example, Southern Illinois University at Edwardsville (SIUE) is working on its recruitment and retention strategies specifically for Black students as a piece of its larger Anti-Racism Taskforce. In looking at the emotional/mental, environmental, and social aspects of wellness, research shows that BIPOC students are more successful when they have a strong sense of community and belonging on campus. In fact, Roksa and Whitley contend that academic motivation can decrease if BIPOC students are only surrounded by white peers.[38] Physical well-being is another key factor in recruiting and retaining BIPOC students. Duc Bo Massey et al.[39] assert that because BIPOC individuals are more susceptible to environmental factors such as extreme weather events, air pollution, and illness, it greatly impacts their ability to be successful in the academy.

What colleges and universities are learning is that it is not only impossible to ignore the eight dimensions of student wellness as they relate to the overall well-being of students, but that it is in fact our job to ensure that resources and support are available to mitigate the environmental and social ramifications of systemic racism. With the emergence of COVID-19 and a rising awareness of the long-term ramifications of systemic racism, college and university libraries have a unique opportunity to be at the forefront of student well-being. Although we have documented many well-being strategies of academic libraries prior to this unprecedented time, there is still much more that we can do.

For example, a group of faculty in Library and Information Services at SIUE is working on a grant to bring underrepresented high school students into library environments for practical work experience as part of their continuing education programs. This will help students to get a broader understanding of the information field, as well as potentially encourage them to pursue library and information science as a profession. Additionally, a group of faculty and staff at both the SIU Edwardsville campus and SIUE's East St. Louis Center are looking at strategies to both recruit and retain BIPOC librarians in the profession. Not only is the profession uncomfortably homogeneous, but it also has a significantly low retention rate for BIPOC individuals due to low morale. Kaetrena Davis Kendrick and Ione T. Damasco[40] contend that low morale is often the cause of dropouts in the library profession and attribute its wide-reaching impact to the fact that BIPOC librarians' conditions in the workplace are amplified by the conditions outside of the workplace, thus making it unbearable.

Given that COVID-19 has put a greater emphasis on health, libraries can use that momentum to continue to provide spaces and services for physical and mental health and even expand those spaces and services. For example, due to a heightened awareness of the transmission of diseases, students may want more options to study independently in contained spaces. While study rooms have long been popular with students, there could be an uptick in demand for them. Because many universities might keep a significant portion of their online offerings even after the pandemic has passed, academic libraries can employ online learning specialists to not only help students but also serve as partners in teaching with other campus faculty.

Conclusion

Prior to 2020, many academic libraries had already been contributing to the holistic well-being of students through nontraditional means. The COVID-19 pandemic and the aftermath of the murder of George Floyd have led to a mental health crisis among college students. Research shows that historically minoritized groups have been impacted even more severely than those with institutionalized privilege by the consequences of COVID-19. This crisis has made it clear, more than ever before, to many universities that they must provide substantive, wide-reaching support for student well-being. As they have begun to plan, a shared understanding of the multi-dimensionality of well-being has begun to emerge.

Though constrained by disruptions to place-based services during the pandemic, academic libraries have creatively responded to these crises by developing a wide range of online resources to promote well-being. Where possible, many libraries have continued to offer physical spaces to meditate, exercise, relax, eat, or socialize. We anticipate that as academic libraries return to full in-person operations they will greatly expand the breadth and diversity of their programs, events, collections, and spaces in order to better address the needs of all students.

As academic libraries invest more time and resources in supporting well-being, we anticipate that they will begin to look more closely at impacts and return on investment. We hope that this will impel libraries to carefully assess the value of their efforts to promote well-being, particularly for minoritized groups. With a commitment to developing an evidence-based approach to helping students flourish, libraries would be able to recognize and adopt best practices. This would enable them to become cornerstones of higher education's well-being success story.

NOTES

1. "The Healthy Minds Study: Fall 2020 Report," Healthy Minds Network, 2021, https://healthymindsnetwork.org/wp-content/uploads/2021/02/HMS-Fall-2020-National-Data-Report.pdf.
2. Maura Mahoney, ed., *Roundtable Report: Creating a Campus Culture of Well-Being* (Washington, DC: Chronicle of Higher Education, 2020).
3. Mahoney, *Roundtable Report*, 9.

4. "The Eight Dimensions of Wellness," William & Mary University, Office of Health & Wellness, www.wm.edu/offices/wellness/about/eight-dimensions/index.php.
5. Meredith Harper Bonham, "College Student Wellness and Mental Health Are Growing Global Issues," *Diverse Issues in Higher Education,* May 30, 2019, https://diverseeducation.com/ article/146841.
6. Healthy Minds Network, "Healthy Minds Study," 3–6.
7. Kat J. McAlpine, "Depression, Anxiety, Loneliness Are Peaking in College Students," *The Brink: Pioneering Research from Boston University* (blog), February 17, 2021, paragraph 8, www.bu.edu/articles/2021/depression-anxiety-loneliness-are-peaking-in-college-students.
8. "Part 3 of 5: Mental Health Impact of COVID-19 on Various Demographic Groups," *Center for Collegiate Mental Health* (blog), February 16, 2021, Penn State University, https://ccmh.psu.edu/index.php?option=com_dailyplanetblog&view=entry&year=2021&month=02&day=15&id=11:part-3-of-5-mental-health-impact-of-covid-19-on-various-demographic-groups.
9. Penn State University, Center for Collegiate Mental Health, "Race/Ethnicity" section, https://ccmh.psu.edu/index.php?option=com_dailyplanetblog&tag=racialethniccultural-concerns.
10. Center for Collegiate Mental Health, "Race/Ethnicity."
11. Center for Collegiate Mental Health, "Race/Ethnicity."
12. Penn State University, Center for Collegiate Mental Health, "Sexual Orientation" section, https://ccmh.psu.edu/index.php?option=com_dailyplanetblog&tag=sexual-orientation.
13. Mahoney, *Roundtable Report,* 20.
14. "Equity in Mental Health Framework: Recommendations for Colleges and Universities to Support the Emotional Well-Being and Mental Health of Students of Color," The Steve Fund and The Jed Foundation, 2017, 3. https://equityinmentalhealth.org/wp-content/uploads/2017/11/Equity-in-Mental-Health-Framework-v17.pdf.
15. Cited in "Equity in Mental Health Framework," 3.
16. Hollie Chessman and Morgan Taylor, *"College Student Mental Health and Well-Being: A Survey of Presidents," Higher Education Today* (blog), August 12, 2019, www.higheredtoday.org/2019/08/12/college-student-mental-health-well-survey-college-presidents.
17. Mahoney, *Roundtable Report.*
18. Mahoney, *Roundtable Report,* 9.
19. Mahoney, *Roundtable Report,* 16.
20. Mahoney, *Roundtable Report,* 21.
21. Mahoney, *Roundtable Report,* 21.

22. Kristin Henrich, "Supporting Student Wellbeing and Holistic Success: A Public Services Approach," *International Information & Library Review* 52, no. 3 (2020): 235, https://doi.org/10.1080/ 10572317.2020.1785171; Elizabeth Ramsey and Mary C. Aagard, "Academic Libraries as Active Contributors to Student Wellness," *College & Undergraduate Libraries* 25, no. 4 (2018): 328–29, https://doi.org/10.1080/ 10691316.2018.1517433.
23. Marta Bladek, "Student Well-Being Matters: Academic Library Support for the Whole Student," *Journal of Academic Librarianship* 47, no. 3, published online March 4, 2021, https://dop.org/10.1016/j.acalib.2021.102349.
24. Ramsey and Aagard, "Academic Libraries."
25. ACRL Research Planning and Review Committee, "2020 Top Trends in Academic Libraries," *College & Research Libraries News* 81, no. 6 (2020), https://crln.acrl.org/index.php/crlnews/ article/view/ 24478/32304.
26. "Moffit Library Rest Zone," University of California Berkeley Libraries, www.lib.berkeley.edu/libraries/moffitt-library/rest-zone.
27. Ramsey and Aagard, "Academic Libraries," 330.
28. Ramsey and Aagard, "Academic Libraries," 331.
29. Coleen Martin, "Take a Study Break during Finals Week," *California State Northridge University Library* (blog), May 6, 2019, https://library.csun.edu/blogs/cited/2019/05/06/take-a-study-break-during-finals-week.
30. Teresa Helena Moreno and Jennifer M. Jackson, "Redefining Student Success in the Academic Library: Building a Critically Engaged Undergraduate Engagement Program," *Research Library Issues* 301 (2020): 6.
31. Moreno and Jackson, "Redefining Student Success," 18.
32. "Wellness Days," Pennsylvania State University, 2021, https://wellnessdays.psu.edu.
33. "Wellness Days Book Club," Pennsylvania State University, paragraph 1, https://sites.psu.edu/librarystudentevents/2021/02/19/interested-in-a-book-club.
34. Randa Lopez Morgan, "Supporting Student Wellness and Success through the LSU Libraries Relaxation Room," *Journal of Library Outreach and Engagement* 1, no. 1 (2020): 104–15, https://doi.org/10.21900/j.jloe.v1i1.469.
35. Morgan, "Supporting Student Wellness," 110.
36. "Wellness at the Libraries," NC State Libraries, n.d., https://www.lib.ncsu.edu/wellness.
37. "Library De-Stress Activities," University of California San Diego Libraries, https://library.ucsd.edu/visit/de-stress.html.
38. Josipa Roksa and Sarah E. Whitley, "Fostering Academic Success of First-Year Students: Exploring the Roles of Motivation, Race, and Faculty," *Journal of College Student Development* 58, no. 3 (2017): 333–48.

39. Melanie Duc Bo Massey, Suchinta Artif, Catalina Albury, and Victoria A. Cluney, "Ecology and Evolutionary Biology Must Elevate BIPOC Scholars," *Ecology Letters* 24 (2021): 913–19.
40. Kaetrena Davis Kendrick and Ione T. Damasco, "Low Morale in Ethnic and Racial Minority Librarians: An Experimental Study," *Library Trends* 68, no. 2 (2019): 174–212.

MICHELLE REALE

Employing the Disenfranchised Student for Mentoring and Empowerment

When I began hiring students almost twenty years ago to work at the access services desk of my university library, I did so in order to fill slots, and to cover crucial times to always ensure that the desk was never empty. Scheduling was, back then, (surprisingly) one of the most complicated aspects of supervising students. No-shows, students who came on strong with enthusiasm but fizzled out early, lateness, incessant rule-breaking, and disrespect were common in my experience. In conversations with my counterparts in our consortium, I found that while most if not all of them experienced the same sort of difficulties, none, as I remember, had the difficulties that I had to the degree which I had them. This puzzled and disturbed me. It was not until I hosted a panel discussion at my institution focused on students and the access services desk that I realized that my approach to the work/life reality of students was way off and needed not just fine-tuning, but an entire overhaul of thinking and feeling on my part. The discussion that day startled me because so much of it was focused on what we, as supervisors, could do for our students, rather than what they could do for us. That day was the start of an entire paradigm shift for me. Yes, obviously we needed the access services desk to run smoothly and be well-staffed. But the issues I was experiencing and the frustrations that went along with it were things that I could remedy by refocusing on the students in a more holistic way and applying an ethic of care to ensure that their library employment (for many their first job, ever) was more than just a satisfactory one.

Previously, I had been focused on the myriad of duties that needed to be done each day, without realizing that from the outside, the access services desk job looked deceptively simple—and therefore, easy, which is why many students sought the position. They quickly and easily became discouraged during training and either quit or just didn't do the things that were expected of them, and I felt more like a den mother than a supervisor. It was a frustrating and time-consuming experience for everyone involved. And I despaired of ever being able to find *capable* students. I didn't see that the problem was not necessarily the students themselves, but more so the way I expected them to "fit right in" and just do as they were asked without guidance that was intentional, ongoing, and which met them where they were at, wherever that was. Many students on college campuses are disenfranchised in one way or another and campus employment, in the form of a library job, can help to address their issues of financial distress, loneliness, and lack of mentoring, among others. I have seen library employment boost students' confidence, give them a satisfying first foray into the world of employment, provide a place in which student employees feel comfortable, and give them the ability to manage their needs and responsibilities better because of some extra added income. Recognizing the student worker in a holistic way helps contribute to their feeling of safety in the world and reinforces that they are more than just their output, in a world that often glorifies the end result, but not necessarily the journey.

That panel discussion helped me to realize, more fully than I ever had before, that all students are capable, but most of them have never held a job before and, for a variety of reasons, have never been encouraged, mentored, or empowered in any way. Many of the students who came to me were struggling with a variety of issues that are common to the college experience, such as being away from home for the first time and missing their parents, the comfort of familiar surroundings, and their best friends—and these often overlapped with other issues such as disenfranchisement and microaggressions due to their color, social or sexual orientation, disability, low economic status, food insecurity, first-generation student status, and other issues. These students needed, for lack of a better way to say it, a *soft place to land* in order to learn *how to be* on and in a job, and they needed caring guidance and mentorship. And a soft place to land is not a place in which excuses are made for students who are not fulfilling the job requirements, but instead a place where fertile ground is cultivated and optimized for learning. We know that learning happens in many different ways and in many different places, but it is our responsibility to prepare the conditions for it with an ethic of care.

While *student engagement* is a phrase that is often heard in higher education, academic libraries have tended to think about it more along the lines of the services and support for academic success they can offer through collection development, technology, learning commons, space, and popular collections, among others.

The early professional literature reveals a lack of focus on the hiring, training, and retention of students in the library as a way of *empowering* them, and sometimes providing them with a place to belong. In one rather jarring example, Gerlich casts a wary eye on student workers in the library, and asserts that "a healthy portion of time and resources are spent trying to convince a rather bored teenager that working in a library is both cool and beneficial."[1] Gerlich goes on to deride the time put into supervising student workers, which "far exceeded the results that student employees contributed to the organization." This perspective views student workers as simply labor, without the attendant ethic of care for who they are as individuals and what kind of experiences they want, and thus it misses a golden opportunity. Gerlich viewed the student solely in terms of output, and while some may still subscribe to that view, we now know how important it is to attend holistically to students' needs, particularly marginalized students who might otherwise be deprived of employment opportunities on campus. I use Gerlich as an example of how far our thinking has evolved with regard to student workers in the library.

Moreover, it is unfair to place all of the blame on the lack of motivation of student workers. Often student workers are deprived of meaningful work that has attendant learning opportunities; this is similar to the experiences many of them have at internships, where they are given little or no guidance, and are either ignored or given work they inherently know is meant to keep them busy, rather than to add anything to the organization. I have heard students describe the work they were asked to do as "meaningless." Creating expectations without proper training and a high tolerance for mistakes while the student is learning creates an environment in which a student may become bored, angry, disincentivized, disinterested, and noncompliant. Those who supervise students in the library have most likely experienced this. Our response may be to dismiss the student in the hope that they will find a job somewhere else that suits them better, but in fact, we should do exactly the opposite: we should take a look at ourselves and examine the conditions and expectations that students have been working under. I have had students tell me they felt unsupported and afraid to reveal that they didn't know (or couldn't remember) something from their training. Marginalized students in the library will perhaps feel this more acutely, as they are already laboring under the assumptions of others about who they are and what their capabilities might be.

Years ago, I hired a student who was in her second year of college, which was a few hours from home. She was one of the quietest students I'd ever encountered. When she did speak, she stuttered. By her own admission, she did not make friends easily. She asked for a shift that virtually no student wanted: our Friday evening shift. I told her she could have those hours (she'd work them with me), but to let me know if she needed to make an adjustment somewhere along the way—hinting that she might want to make plans for a Friday night in the future. "That won't happen," she said nonchalantly, a seemingly blasé comment that made me think. She was planting her feet in the position. She was amazingly detailed, conscientious, and had wonderful customer service skills, which landed her a supervisory position much quicker than what is normal in my library. She was receptive to learning things and showed a lot of initiative, which was amazing. The library on Friday nights was as quiet as one would expect it to be, so she was able to learn a lot of the basics of the job without pressure. She felt comfortable and welcomed, which I believe helped her to build her own confidence as she grew into the position and made it her own. She began expressing more enthusiasm for her classes and stopped expressing the nearly constant desire to go home for the weekend (six hours away) which she had been consistently focused on. She told me she had never thought she would like library work, and said she was surprised that there was so much to it. While I had hoped (and admittedly, tried to steer her in that direction) that she would consider librarianship as a career, she told me that she "couldn't think that far ahead." *Fair enough.* She worked Friday nights in the library until she graduated. I would say that the young girl who asked to work Friday nights in the library was vastly different from the mature young woman I watched graduate. Strayhorn calls this "belonging," and defines it thus:

> In terms of college, a sense of belonging refers to students' perceived social support on campus, a feeling or sensation of connectedness, and the experience of mattering or feeling cared about, accepted, respected, valued by, and important to the campus community or others on campus such as faculty, staff, and peers.[2]

With regard to faculty-student interactions, a sense of belonging on the part of the student matters in so many ways. Cook-Sather and Felten identify three dynamic processes that converge to create an "enhanced sense of belonging": these are "doing meaningful work together, creating spaces and opportunities for exploration and growth, and engaging in regular and ongoing affirmation of all involved."[3] A holistic, ethic-of-care approach can make students feel as though they belong and can create conditions that make belonging not just a perception, though the perception is essential for a sense of well-being, but also a reality.

We can view the employment of students in the library as faculty-student engagement if, and only if, we engage in the development of the students by regular and meaningful interaction with them. A by-product of this kind of engagement with the student is, of course, our own development as caring and intentional individuals and educators.

What does this engagement look like in practice? For me, it started with prioritizing and centering the needs of those who expressed feelings of marginalization and disenfranchisement in the course of one-on-one interviews—as was evident when an older student would apply for a position and mention that they were a single-parent commuter with small children. One student had left her small child with her parents back in North Dakota to be able to study in one of our programs. She told me that she was currently the only Native American student on campus, and that our East Coast campus was vastly different from "the reservation back home." She was a wonderful addition to our staff and was incredibly capable, and showed a lot of initiative. I gave her a lot of feedback, and created an environment of trust which it took her a bit of time to settle into, but eventually, settle she did. Another student, one on the autism spectrum, confided in me one day that he felt continually misunderstood at the access services desk and that the interactions with students and others were incredibly stressful for him. One of the main jobs at that desk is customer service. I needed someone to take an inventory of our academic reserves and all that it entailed, including keeping detailed records in the form of spreadsheets, and this worked out perfectly for him.

There is a fine balance between this sort of mentoring, on the one hand, and allowing the student to learn new skills in their own way without feeling as though they are constantly being watched, on the other. Cook-Sather and Felten recognize this as a sort of liminal space where what is possible is a "balanced give-and-take not of commodities but of perspectives."[4] Once a supervisor shows an ethic of care (and finding solutions and the "right fit" for a student are included in that ethic), the student comes to feel that they are working within a framework of learning. This is the opposite of a *transactional* relationship—the hiring of a student for their labor only. When we think of campus employment as an extension of learning which in reality is not all that different from what occurs in the classroom, we open up new vistas and opportunities for students. This gives us the opportunity to create spaces for students who have none of their own, and give them the feeling of belonging that is often missing from their experiences.

Staff and faculty alike will bemoan the lack of time in our workaday lives to be able to mentor and attend to the whole student, but if we frame campus employment as an extension of the classroom (which it is), we come to understand that not attending to students is a sort of dereliction of duty. While they are not particular to libraries, Kuh et al. list six characteristics from the ten "high-impact practices" developed by the Association of American Colleges & Universities that are designed to "increase rates of student retention and student engagement."[5] Rinto, Mitola, and Otto assert that "part-time student employment in the library can offer another mechanism in which students gain the benefits of High-Impact Practices, if those student employment programs are designed with student learners in mind."[6] In my own experience, it has not been an easy task to carefully mentor students and make sure that their work environment is healthy and supportive, but this will not stop me from consistently trying.

My experience has been that the same students get consistently chosen for opportunities on campus, which replicates what various students have told me about their high school experiences where they felt unseen. Being attuned to students who, for whatever reason, consider themselves "off center stage" will help to elevate them, create the potential for new opportunities, and help them feel empowered in their lives. Cook-Sather and Porte recognize that it is "the combination of transparent emotional commitment and theory that awakens academic spaces and leaves room for different forms of engagement."[7] We need to be consistently intentional in our hiring practices and follow-through for the disenfranchised and marginalized student. It takes work and commitment to expand our notion of what is possible, to draw in and include those who are habitually ignored or disregarded. This vision seeks to look past what the Nigerian author Chimamanda Ngozi Adichie has called the "single story." In a class that I teach on refugees, the first day always includes a viewing of Adichie's TED Talk "The Dangers of a Single Story." She warns against forming stereotypes and assumptions about people based on only one aspect of them, be it their economic status, color, or disability, and she explains how and why it is limiting and dangerous to do so. My students are always thrown a bit off-balance by this video, and experience both guilt and confusion as I ask them what assumptions they harbor about different groups of people. In the video, Adichie forcefully counters stereotypes and assumptions thus: "The single story creates stereotypes, and the problem with stereotypes is not that they are untrue, *but that they are incomplete*. They make one story become *the only story*"[8] (emphases mine).

For generations, people have found refuge and comfort in libraries of all kinds. For disenfranchised students, the library has the potential to become a powerful place to grow through caring mentorship; it can be a place to thrive, and enjoy freedom from various kinds of oppression they experience, and this in turn has the potential to help them build resilience, connections, and competencies that will help them in so many ways in the future.

NOTES

1. Bella Karr Gerlich, "Rethinking the Contributions of Student Employees to Library Services," *Library Administration and Management* 16, no. 3 (2002): 146–50.
2. Terrell L. Strayhorn, *College Students' Sense of Belonging: A Key to Educational Success for All Students* (New York: Routledge, 2018), 3, https://doi.org/10.4324/9781315297293.
3. Alison Cook-Sather and Peter Felten, "Where Student Engagement Meets Faculty Development: How Student-Faculty Pedagogical Partnership Fosters a Sense of Belonging," *Student Engagement in Higher Education Journal* 1, no. 2 (2017): 3–11.
4. Alison Cook-Sather and Peter Felten, "Ethics of Academic Leadership: Guiding Learning and Teaching," in *Cosmopolitan Perspectives on Academic Leadership in Higher Education,* ed. Feng Su and Margaret Wood (London: Bloomsbury Academic, 2017), 175–91.
5. George D. Kuh, Jillian L. Kinzie, Jennifer A. Buckley, Brian K. Bridges, and John C. Hayek, "What Matters to Student Success: A Review of the Literature," National Postsecondary Education Cooperative, 2006.
6. Erin Rinto, Rosan Mitola, and Kate Otto, "Reframing Library Student Employment as a High-Impact Practice: Implications from Case Studies," *College & Undergraduate Libraries* 26, no. 4 (2019): 260–77.
7. Alison Cook-Sather and Olivia Porte, "Reviving Humanity: Grasping within and beyond Our Reach," *Journal of Educational Innovation, Partnership and Change* 3, no. 1 (2017): 299–302.
8. Chimamanda Ngozi Adichie, "The Danger of a Single Story," 2009, TED Talk, www.ted.com/talks/chimamanda_ngozi_adichie_the_danger_of_a_single_story.

Part III
Libraries Providing Financial Support

FELICIA A. SMITH

Loving Libraries
Stanford University Library's Paid Summer Internships

> Success is to be measured not so much by the position that one has reached in life as by the obstacles which he has overcome while trying to succeed.
> —Booker T. Washington

The Stanford University Libraries partnered with Eastside College Preparatory School in East Palo Alto, California, in 2013–14 to provide paid summer internships to local, aspiring, first-generation college students who were low-income and members of underrepresented minority groups. The summer internships typically lasted from June through August, with a main goal of providing the interns with paid job experiences while also exposing them to key aspects of college life, especially the crucial role of libraries in student success. Our overarching goal was to create successful students who *"love libraries!"*

Our first cohort of interns, in the summer of 2013, included six recent Eastside high school graduates and one Eastside high school sophomore. Our second cohort of interns, in the summer of 2014, included six recent Eastside high school graduates and four Eastside juniors. All of our interns were the first in their families to attend college. In addition to providing these students with well-paying summer jobs in the Stanford libraries, our program included weekly enrichment activities designed to increase the interns' awareness of key sources of support that would be available at their colleges.

Background

East Palo Alto was chosen specifically because of the presence of our target demographic as well as the systematic disinvestment in that area, which spanned decades. For example, this area did not have banking facilities or even a supermarket—its only bank branch shut down in 1988. In 2018, the local PBS affiliate reported that an ATM machine was the only major bank presence in East Palo Alto, a city of nearly 30,000 residents. In addition to the lack of services in the area, a 1992 crime wave brought East Palo Alto notoriety as America's per-capita murder capital.[1]

More of the area's tragic history is recounted on the Eastside school website: "When East Palo Alto's only high school closed in 1976, students were bused to high schools in neighboring, more affluent towns. The results were dramatic: 65% of students from East Palo Alto dropped out of high school, and less than 10% enrolled in four-year colleges."[2] The Stanford graduate Chris Bischof founded Eastside College Preparatory School in 1996, and his school understandably boasts about their remarkable results: "Eighty percent of our alumni are either in a four-year college or have graduated, in comparison with a sobering nationwide statistic indicating that just 11% of first-generation college students graduate from college."[3]

Even though Bischof received his master's degree in education from Stanford's Teacher Education Program, this was not the main reason why we decided to work with his school. His school is conveniently located just four miles away from Stanford University's main campus, and as previously mentioned, the demographics of the school and its community were included in the thoughtful justification that went into selecting students from that specific area.

Logistics

Several personal opportunities afforded to me as a young professional guided the internship program I would later create at Stanford University. As a first-generation low-income college student, I benefited greatly from having a paid summer INROADS internship throughout college that provided me with real-life corporate experience as well as intensive training. INROADS' mission is to develop and place talented minority youth in business and industry and prepare them for corporate and community leadership. In 1970, founder Frank Carr recognized systemic racial disparities in society and decided to take meaningful actions to reduce them. The INROADS website states: "It's no secret that for years, people of color—Blacks, Hispanic/Latinos, and Native American Indians—were noticeably absent from the ranks of corporate America."[4]

I was subsequently honored to serve as a mentor for high school students while I was a librarian-in-residence at the University of Notre Dame. Mentoring was an important component of the university's Project to Recruit the Next Generation of Librarians internship for recent high school graduates. Mentors volunteered to advise the summer interns on strategies for success as prospective college students. Mentors were assigned to one or more students and met two hours per week for a minimum of sixteen hours over the eight weeks of the internship.[5]

The aforementioned are just a couple of experiences that helped shape my participation in the internship program at Stanford University Libraries, and I sincerely hope these successful examples will inspire others to make a change in the lives of future generations, no matter how small.

After I proposed the internship program, Stanford Libraries secured funding for it mainly by using salary savings from vacant faculty positions. After confirming there was enough money to hire high school students and pay them more than the minimum wage, we contacted the Eastside College Preparatory School and asked if they would be interested in partnering with Stanford University Libraries to provide paid internships for their students.

One measurable goal of the internship was to expose low-income and underrepresented minority high-school students to the library science profession in a university setting. We planned to achieve that goal by increasing the interns' awareness of library and information science as a professional career option by giving them real-life work experience. We instructed the interns on how to conduct college-level research, and we emphasized ways for them to develop financial literacy skills that they would be able to use in everyday life as undergraduates.

The interns were required to be at least sixteen years old and must have completed their freshman year of high school before starting the internship. All interns were required to be college-bound. Preference was given to students who had been accepted to, or who had applied to, Stanford University. Two interns were incoming Stanford University students, and they both continued to work for the university libraries during Stanford's academic school year.

Preference was also given to students from low-income families and/or students who expected to be first-generation college students. Eastside's student population is 78 percent Latinx, 18 percent African American, and 4 percent Pacific Islander.

There were a lot of logistics involved in these internships, and the work schedules required constant flexibility. Each intern was supervised by a Stanford University Libraries staff member. Exact work schedules were determined by the specific needs of participating library departments and the availability of the respective intern. The internships were scheduled from June until August. Interns were scheduled to work forty hours per week, with at least one hour per week devoted to an enrichment activity. The hours spent in enrichment activities counted as work hours, and the interns were paid for that enrichment time. We were pleased to be able to offer the interns more than the minimum wage.

Sample jobs included:

- Inventory items in our technology department
- Inventory the manuscript and archival collections
- Serials preservation
- Inspect and reshelve our 78 RPM recordings collection

Enrichment activities included:

- Social skills, presentation software skills, leadership, public speaking, and networking
- Information literacy workshops, including ones on library databases and online catalogs
- Introduction to Photoshop, video-editing, and multimedia software

Weekly training sessions focused on professionalism and overall etiquette, including social networks visibility, personal outgoing voicemail messages on their phones, using formal titles when addressing coworkers, and so on. We also had to address the topic of proper business attire. The interns gained exposure to a wide variety of career options during their tours of campus departments.

As a reward for their hard work, we took the interns on field trips and tours that reinforced our training messages and allowed them to have fun with their coworkers and build relationships. The most popular team-building activity, by far, was their visit to Stanford's Virtual Human Interaction Lab. There they each took part, individually, in an immersive virtual reality environment complete with headgear, hand sensors, and powerful surround-sound with built-in wall panels consisting of 24 channels of 360-degree sound, along with haptic floors that have 16 subwoofers underneath. The most popular off-campus outing was laser tag. The off-campus outings were complicated by policies requiring parents' travel consent forms to transport minors away from campus.

At the end of the internships, each intern cohort created a final presentation, part of which was a video that they created and edited completely on their own and published on one of their personal websites.

The interns' exit interviews showed that in addition to the enrichment activities, they really enjoyed the motivational guest speakers, and their introduction to college software and resources. Their high school did not have a library, so the information literacy and digital literacy instruction was incredibly beneficial.

Lessons Learned

Even though these types of internships are well-meaning, there have been lessons learned along the way. One example that I learned from was one university's illogical restriction which prohibited its students from obtaining student employment until after they had paid all their school fees. I called the interns to see how they were adjusting to college life, and that was when one student told me they hadn't been able to get the student job at the university library that we had arranged for them. They could not apply for the job because they owed over $600 in school fees when they started college, and this student absolutely could not afford to pay these fees. But until the fees were paid, our former intern could not get a student job and therefore could not earn money. Even if the students had known this during their internship, I doubt they could have afforded to set aside hundreds of dollars in anticipation of this financial obstacle. I asked the student for their account information, and then I logged on and charged their school fees on my credit card. One of my colleagues, Adan Griego, voluntarily donated $150 toward the intern's fees. Adan's selflessness and magnanimity are examples of the desirable character traits that our most successful managers possess. We were lucky to have so many truly dedicated managers who worked tirelessly to provide emotional as well as financial support for our cherished interns. The intern reported soon afterward that they did finally start working in the library job we had arranged for them during the summer. When prearranging a student job, the library staff should confirm with their contacts at the intern's university whether any such financial requirements exist.

None of the interns ever shared their financial struggles related to transportation with their managers or with me as the program coordinator. We finally learned a little about these financial difficulties because library staff observed one intern walking a long distance to work. This intern was walking at least five miles, or approximately 1.5 hours, each way to and from campus every day. Interestingly, most of our information about financial struggles came after the interns confided in one of our non-Stanford college student workers, Veronica Rubalcava, who served as the interns' liaison and as my assistant coordinator. The students felt incredibly comfortable talking to Rubalcava, who was only a couple of years older than they. Rubalcava proved elemental in helping make the internships successful. She provided invaluable insights into the obstacles the interns faced without betraying their confidence. It made sense that they would not feel comfortable complaining to their managers about issues they had with their job, such as transportation.

Because Rubalcava was a newly hired student worker, she was also invaluable in helping to allay the fears of many interns about completing their employment paperwork from Human Resources. The interns had deep-rooted concerns that their paperwork could lead to raids of their homes by Immigration and Customs Enforcement. Rubalcava's position was designed to give a non-Stanford college student from a minority group a paid job that would provide her with professional marketable experience. Rubalcava had the perfect personality for this job, even though this was her first time working in a business setting, too. She could relate to what the interns were going through, and she could also help the interns understand their managers' perspectives and company procedures.

Sensitivity and empathy are crucial components of a successful internship. The interns got along well with their managers, but they were not comfortable asking for additional financial help. As I mentioned earlier, a few interns were spotted walking great distances to get to work. Others were trying to use their salary to help pay for gas because family members drove them to work daily. I later found out that a handful of interns were racking up parking tickets at a nearby mall because they could not afford to buy campus parking permits. Even though the amount of their parking tickets was far greater than the price of permits, the due date for the ticket violations was in the future. Once again, we relied on Rubalcava to inform us about these previously unforeseen expenses. After we were made aware of these expenditures, we immediately purchased parking permits for all of those who drove to work, and we provided bus fare to the others.

Luckily, we had the foresight to plan for the high cost of meals, on campus and in the surrounding area. To reduce the amount of money interns needed to spend on food, we scheduled lunches once a week that were paid for by either the library or by their managers. If the interns were attending a mandatory training session, the library paid the bill for lunch. We frequently invited Stanford's staff from different departments to join our group lunches. We focused on staff members who were first-generation college students or were from low-income families or minority communities. The interns loved these sessions because they gained valuable advice from highly successful people, who were also just like them.

One extremely important group that met with our interns was the First-Gen and/or Low Income (FLI) Office staff. The director of FLI treated our interns to lunch at Stanford's fancy faculty club after giving them a tour of the FLI offices and sharing all of the wonderful services that they provide. FLI staff also pointed out their counterparts at each of the interns' prospective universities. The interns were thrilled to learn that there are organizations like FLI dedicated to supporting them with money, similar to Stanford's Opportunity Fund, which covers expenses such as:

- Travel costs related to a death or illness
- Citizenship fees
- Laptop repair or replacement in the event of an emergency, up to $1,000
- Medical/dental expenses
- Attending conferences/workshops, up to $1,000
- Assistance with professional clothing, up to $250

Conclusion

In addition to weekly group lunches, we strongly encouraged each manager to take their intern to lunch at least once every two weeks, as a way to provide free meals for the interns without making them feel like charity cases. These manager lunches were encouraged as networking opportunities. Managers often treated the interns to lunch together so they could feel more relaxed in the buddy system. After the interns got comfortable with the library staff, and after some tips from guest speakers, the interns were more conversant in workplace dialogue. I did ask managers to balance the number of manager lunches with allowing the interns the opportunity to stop and unwind away from library staff over their lunch hours.

As I stated earlier, sensitivity and empathy were crucial responses to the financial strains our interns were under. Unfortunately, I was completely oblivious to one episode of mental and emotional distress that was affecting them. I spent so much of the first month of the internship focused on providing an enriching curriculum for them that I completely overlooked a high-profile, racially charged event in the news that was impacting their mental well-being. My oversight was remedied during our 2013 enrichment event, which featured Stanford's former dean of freshmen and undergraduate advising, Julie Lythcott-Haims, who was affectionately called "Dean Julie." The first thing she asked the interns was "What is on your minds/hearts?" As previously stated, this group had not been very forthcoming about personal issues, except with Rubalcava, so I was completely flabbergasted when they all immediately shared with Dean Julie their gut-wrenching fears and palpable anxieties after watching the newly released movie *Fruitvale Station*, a film about the police killing of Oscar Grant in a nearby city. Their racial trauma from watching this film was so all-encompassing that I was stunned that they had all hidden their pain so well. There was not a dry eye in the room. Luckily, in addition to the cleansing catharsis of unexpected tears, there was lots of laughter.

Our Stanford University Libraries' internship program was focused on creating successful students, with transferable skills, who love libraries. I am confident in claiming, "Mission Accomplished!"

I would be remiss if I did not mention that the internships ended because of university-wide budgetary constraints. Nevertheless, one of my coworkers recommended that we restart our internship program as a library response to the murder of George Floyd. Unfortunately, occupancy limitations because of the COVID-19 pandemic have delayed the project, but library staff are working with dedicated people like Adan Griego to revise and adapt the internship for relaunch ideally in 2022.

In closing, I would like to encourage others to do whatever they can, no matter how small, to help students get financial assistance and emotional support along their knowledge-seeking journey. The best way I can say this is: *"Being inspired as an intern was great, but inspiring the next generation of interns is true greatness."*

NOTES

1. Tonya Mosley, "'It's Like a Tax for Living in East Palo Alto': Life in a Bank Desert," KQED, 2018, www.kqed.org/news/11679947/its-like-a-tax-for-living-in-east-palo-alto-life-in-a-bank-desert.
2. Chris Bischof, "Eastside College Preparatory School's History," Eastside College Preparatory School, www.eastside.org/_about/history.html.
3. Bischof, "Eastside College Preparatory School's History."
4. Frank Carr, "INROADS History," INROADS, https://inroads.org/about-inroads/history-mission/.
5. Dwight King, "The Next Generation: Partnering with High Schools for Future Minority Librarians," *College & Research Libraries News* 4, no. 71 (2010): 201, https://doi.org/10.5860/crln.71.4.8356.

ZARA WILKINSON

Throwing the University Wide Open

Textbook Affordability and COVID-19

Textbook affordability has become a rallying cry in higher education in the United States, and libraries have been leading the charge. In the name of affordability, countless college and university libraries have launched initiatives that encourage teaching faculty to stop relying on expensive commercial textbooks and adopt free online course materials instead. These initiatives typically focus on the potential academic and financial impact on students, as well as the potential for pedagogical innovation by faculty who redevelop their courses with affordability in mind. While these textbook affordability initiatives have already spread across the country and benefited thousands of students, they took on new importance when the COVID-19 pandemic forced colleges and universities to severely limit or cease in-person operations. This chapter discusses the significance of textbook affordability initiatives, taking as a case study the Open and Affordable Textbooks (OAT) program at Rutgers University and the increased interest in the program due to the pandemic.

The Affordability Crisis

Between 1977 and 2015, the price of college and university tuition increased at a rate two times greater than that of inflation, but even this was far outpaced by the increase in the price of textbooks.[1] In fact, a commonly cited NBC analysis of Bureau of Labor Statistics data found that textbook prices rose at a rate three times greater than the rate of inflation during the period.[2] Thus, while there is mounting concern about the affordability of higher education in general, considerable attention has also been focused on the burden that textbook costs place on students. In a 2018 survey of 20,000 Florida Virtual Campus students, for example, 64 percent indicated that they had been unable to purchase at least one textbook due to its price.[3] National surveys conducted by the Student Public Interest Research Groups in 2014 and 2020 yielded similar results.[4] In both surveys, at least 90 percent of students who went without a textbook worried that doing so would hinder their ability to succeed in the course. From this it is clear that many students are not cavalierly opting to forego their textbooks; rather, they are being forced to make a purely financial decision despite their concerns about the consequences.

While costly textbooks are or might be an impediment for many students, textbook affordability is an even more pressing issue for historically underserved students. Rising textbook costs may particularly affect low-income, first-generation, and first-year students,[5] as well as students of color generally.[6] These same student populations already face lower rates of retention and graduation. Studies have documented a persistent gap in completion rates between low-income students and their high-income peers,[7] and between first-generation students and students whose parents earned a bachelor's degree.[8] Graduation rates also vary by race and ethnicity: a report issued by the National Center for Education Statistics found that Black, Latinx, and American Indian students have the lowest rates of college completion.[9] Textbook costs represent one more hurdle placed between students such as these, who are already more vulnerable than their peers, and the successful completion of a college degree.

A growing awareness of the negative impact that textbook costs have on students' ability to meet their educational goals has led to what has been called a "textbook revolution."[10] Colleges and universities across the United States have sought ways to reduce the financial burden placed on the shoulders of their students. At most of these institutions, textbook affordability efforts have been located in the library system, leveraging libraries' strengths in promoting student success and supporting classroom instruction. At some libraries, affordability has focused on physical course reserves and textbook purchasing,[11] or on access to e-textbooks through the library.[12] One of the most effective ways that libraries have responded to the textbook affordability crisis, however, is the implementation of specific initiatives designed to incentivize the use of open educational resources (OER), open textbooks, and other affordable or free course materials.

A common model is one in which the library offers teaching faculty a small financial grant or stipend in exchange for redesigning a course so that the textbooks used are free or low-cost for students. This is a program design that can be traced to early adopters such as the University of Massachusetts Amherst and the University of California at Los Angeles.[13] Programs such as these offer academic as well as financial benefits to students. The use of open and affordable course materials such as open textbooks has been associated with positive academic impact such as lower rates of D, F, and withdrawal grades, particularly for members of underserved minority groups, Pell Grant recipients, and part-time students.[14]

The OAT Program at Rutgers University

Founded in 1766, Rutgers, the State University of New Jersey, is a public land-grant university with a long and storied history. Today, Rutgers boasts a presence in all of New Jersey's 21 counties and operates four main locations that span the state and collectively serve over 71,000 students from New Jersey, all 50 states, and more than 125 countries. The three main campuses are Rutgers University-Camden, Rutgers University-Newark, and Rutgers University-New Brunswick, each of which offers complete undergraduate and graduate programs in a variety of disciplines; along with Rutgers Biomedical and Health Sciences, which has two medical schools as well schools of nursing, dentistry, pharmacy, and public health. While in many ways these campuses of the university operate independently of each other, they share a common university infrastructure and a variety of central services. One of these central services is the unified library system, Rutgers University Libraries, which stretches across the state to operate all libraries at Rutgers except for those affiliated with the law school.

In 2016, student activists prompted the University Senate to recommend that the university president, then Robert Barchi, create a textbook affordability initiative. President Barchi turned to the University Libraries as a natural home for a program with the potential to impact every part of the university, and so the Open and Affordable Textbooks program was formed. Known colloquially as OAT, the program was designed to directly reduce textbook costs for students. OAT, which is run annually, encourages faculty members to adopt open and affordable course materials such as open textbooks, electronic course reserves, library-licensed materials, and other freely available but not open materials. Each year, teaching faculty are invited to apply to redesign a specific course, usually with the goal of replacing one or more of the commercial textbooks used in the course. The course materials for redesigned OAT courses are usually free to students, but they can sometimes carry a low price tag if there are specific materials which cannot be replaced by a free alternative. In addition to answering a few narrative questions about their redesign plans, faculty members' applications must include the estimated number of students enrolled in the course within the award cycle (generally summer to summer), as well as the amount of money that students will save when the course redesign is completed.

Since the 2016 program launch, OAT has produced an estimated student savings of $6 million for approximately 38,500 students across all Rutgers campuses. Moreover, a survey of students enrolled in OAT courses showed that they found that the redesigned course materials were easier to access, read, take notes on, and use to collaborate.[15] Faculty who redesigned and taught OAT courses also responded positively to a one-time survey of their experiences and reported that their students were prepared, engaged, and achieved learning outcomes to the same or greater degree as when using commercial textbooks.[16] Faculty participants have also indicated that participating in OAT served as an opportunity to make their course content more dynamic, current, and representative of diverse voices.[17] For all of these reasons, the University Libraries consider the program to be a phenomenal success and plan to both continue supporting it and explore ways to build on its accomplishments.

The COVID-19 Crisis and Textbook Affordability

The onset of the COVID-19 pandemic affected every aspect of life in the United States, including the higher education landscape. During the spring 2020 semester, due to public health guidance and government restrictions, many colleges and universities pivoted to entirely online instruction. Campus libraries either closed their doors or scaled back their hours, services, and access to collections. This unprecedented change in both the modality of instruction and availability of campus resources threw into stark relief the challenges many students face in accessing their course materials. With libraries closed, print course reserves discontinued or delayed by quarantine procedures, and social distancing requirements in place, many students were unable to use existing support structures and their tried-and-true strategies for masking their inability to purchase their textbooks. As a result, teaching faculty became keenly (and in some cases, newly) aware that students' inability to afford their required course materials was negatively impacting their ability to achieve academic success.

The interplay between the COVID-19 pandemic and textbook affordability, however, goes far beyond the relatively short-term impact of the virus mitigation efforts. For example, the pandemic has laid bare the existence of the "digital divide"—the reality that while some people enjoy unfettered access to appropriate hardware and broadband internet, many others do not.[18] Increasingly, the digital divide is characterized not by technology ownership, but by the ability to sustain needed levels of access, or "technology maintenance."[19] The divide is well known to split along racial/ethnic and socioeconomic lines, since people of color and low-income households are less likely to have broadband internet at home and are more likely to depend on cell phones.[20] Higher education is not immune to this trend. Low-income students and students of color are more likely than their peers to struggle to maintain access to working technology.[21] A spring 2020 student survey at two Big Ten universities found that 19 percent of students were experiencing technological hardships that impeded their online learning during the COVID-19 pandemic, with higher numbers observed among lower-income students and students of color.[22] National surveys during the same period found a similar trend,[23] with one survey establishing that 1 in 5 college students lacked either a laptop or reliable access to the internet.[24]

The far-reaching financial impact of the COVID-19 pandemic is likely to make it more difficult for students to afford their textbooks and maintain their access to sufficient levels of technology. The pandemic led to staggering unemployment rates, the highest the country had seen since the Great

Depression.²⁵ At some points during the pandemic, nearly half of all adults in the United States lived in households that experienced a loss of employment income.²⁶ Even as the economy improved in early 2021, the United States had 8.5 million fewer jobs in February 2021 than in the same month in 2020, with higher rates of unemployment for women and people of color.²⁷ Students too suffered from the economic downtown: 58 percent of over 38,000 students surveyed in the spring of 2020 experienced some type of basic needs insecurity.²⁸ Many lost their jobs or faced lower wages and reduced hours due to the pandemic,²⁹ reflecting national rates of job losses for young adults.³⁰ At four-year universities like Rutgers, students experienced higher than usual rates of food insecurity (38 percent), housing insecurity (41 percent), and homelessness (15 percent).³¹ In line with national trends, these insecurities were more prevalent among students of color.³²

The economic impact of COVID-19 is likely to continue to affect students and prospective students via their families' finances. Roughly half of all adults believe that they will need three or more years to recover from the financial impact of COVID-19, and some believe they will never recover.³³ It is logical to assume that many more families, even those that would have had the means to do so prior to the pandemic, will struggle to send their children to college. Students who have experienced individual or family financial hardship during COVID-19 may be forced to take on more loans just to get to campus, potentially compounding the racial disparities already documented in the presence and degree of educational debt.³⁴ Additionally, parents' financial health can impact a student's educational attainment, since there is evidence that family debt at the time of applying to college is associated with lower rates of graduation, especially for families of color.³⁵ And since the students most likely to be disadvantaged by the economic fallout of the pandemic are the same students already statistically more likely to be negatively affected by the rising cost of textbooks, textbook affordability initiatives are likely to take on new importance in the wake of COVID-19.

OAT and COVID-19

On March 10, 2020, Rutgers announced that it, like many other universities, would be making the unpreceded shift to remote instruction. The university announced an early start to spring break in order to provide teaching faculty members with a few extra days to prepare for the shift. On March 21, 2020, the New Jersey governor issued an executive order closing all college and university libraries in the state. As a result, the libraries at Rutgers were forced to close their doors, send faculty and staff home to telecommute, and reevaluate all their services in light of the sudden and complete lack of access to print collections. Some library services, such as reference and instruction, could be transitioned to the virtual environment fairly easily while others, such as lending, print course reserves, and interlibrary loan, were forced to cease.

After the university announced the switch to remote instruction, the OAT team became concerned about the spring 2020 application deadline for fall semester course redesign, which had been set at March 30, 2020. But far from worrying about these potential future courses, teaching faculty were suddenly forced to completely redesign their *current* courses to fit the online environment. In some cases, the learning curve was quite steep: many instructors had never taught online or from home, and some had never used any of the university's several learning management systems. The faculty at Rutgers were not alone in this; a study of faculty across the United States found that 93 percent of them made at least one change to their teaching during the shift to online course delivery, and two-thirds of them made substantive changes to their assignments or exams.[36] In order to accommodate these already overtaxed faculty (as well as the University Libraries' own faculty and staff, who were also navigating the transition to working from home), the OAT team and the libraries' leadership decided to extend the OAT deadline by just over a month, leaving applications due on the last day of (online) classes, May 4, 2020.

The updated timeline meant that many faculty were receiving notices about the deadline extension while watching their students struggle with the transition to remote instruction, the inaccessibility of campus resources, and personal financial and health crises, all of which impacted their ability to obtain their required course materials. Due to the timing and an increasing university-wide focus on student hardship, OAT received a record number of applications from instructors for course redesigns for the fall semester. Although university budgets were also tightening, the University

Libraries were able to redirect central funding to the OAT program, enabling the OAT team to increase the number of available awards. Even after doing so, many high-quality applications remained unfunded, so the library directors on each campus were asked to consider sponsoring awards from their local budgets. As a result of this additional central and local funding, the OAT program was able to give more than twice the number of awards originally planned: 42 instead of 20. The spring 2020 awards alone impacted 16,000 students across the university, generating over $2 million in student savings in a single year. In comments published in *Rutgers Today* along with the announcement of the awardees, University Librarian Krisellen Maloney noted the libraries' commitment to supporting students through a difficult period: "With the ongoing pandemic putting financial pressures on so many families, it is more important than ever to do what we can to keep our students' education affordable."[37]

Rutgers University Libraries hopes to build on this momentum and continue the success of OAT. In 2021, the libraries opened applications for the sixth round of the OAT program, with an increased emphasis on diversity, equity, and inclusion (DEI). The OAT team added a new "DEI" category to its evaluation rubric and specifically asked applicants to discuss how their project promoted DEI, whether in terms of course content, delivery, or accessibility. Because OAT was designed to reduce financial barriers that perpetuate inequality, DEI has always been a core component of the program. However, an intentional and explicit focus on DEI felt particularly necessary after the uneven impact of the COVID-19 pandemic and the civil unrest due to racial injustices and police brutality that marked 2020.[38] This was coupled with the incoming university president, Jonathan Holloway, bringing with him a focus on DEI that included a university equity audit and the appointment of a senior vice president for equity.

In 2021, the Libraries also expanded their existing textbook affordability efforts by piloting a new Authoring Award, which offers a larger sum ($3,500) for writing a complete open textbook. Although the OAT program has always included authoring a new resource among its options for faculty who receive awards, the explicit focus on OER creation is a new direction for Rutgers University Libraries. This award aims to diversify the options available to instructors by supporting the creation of open textbooks on topics underserved by existing OER materials. The Libraries originally planned to select only one faculty member for the first year of this new award, but ultimately the OAT team elected to recommend that additional awards be funded due to the breadth and quality of the applications received. In total, four faculty members received an Authoring Award, representing Rutgers-New Brunswick, Rutgers-Camden, and Rutgers Biomedical and Health Sciences.

Conclusion

The COVID-19 pandemic will have a far-reaching impact in the years to come. Many Americans will continue to suffer from the economic ramifications of massive job losses and crippled service industries. Current trends suggest that these ramifications will be felt unequally, with low-income families and families of color experiencing a disproportionate degree of hardship. As the students in these families reach higher education, these inequities will affect the universities they choose or can afford, the amount of debt they will need to take on, their ability to attend full-time and/or study without working, and their ability to afford the many non-tuition costs of college such as housing, meal plans, and required textbooks. Furthermore, relatively little is known about the long-term impact of other pandemic-related policy decisions, such as the closure of primary and secondary schools, which may exacerbate existing academic and social inequalities for students with disabilities or from low-income communities.[39] After the COVID pandemic has passed, DEI and affordability initiatives will be even more vital in ensuring that colleges and universities are admitting, educating, and graduating students from all backgrounds. While textbook prices are only one element of college affordability, the affordability of textbooks is a relatively easy issue for academic libraries to address. Many libraries already have programs supporting the adoption of open and affordable course materials and providing education about course reserves, OER, and other ways that faculty can reduce costs for students. The success of programs such as the Open and Affordable Textbooks initiative at Rutgers University demonstrates that faculty are interested in participating in textbook affordability initiatives, and they may be primed for participation after watching their students experience hardship during the COVID-19 pandemic.

NOTES

1. Joseph A. Salem Jr., "Open Pathways to Student Success: Academic Library Partnerships for Open Educational Resource and Affordable Course Content Creation and Adoption," *Journal of Academic Librarianship* 43, no. 1 (2017): 34–38.
2. Ben Popken, "College Textbook Prices Have Risen 1,041 Percent Since 1977," *NBC News*, 2015, www.nbcnews.com/feature/freshman-year/college-textbook-prices-have-risen-812-percent-1978-n399926.
3. "2018 Student Textbook and Course Materials Survey," Florida Virtual Campus, 2019, 3, https://dlss.flvc.org/colleges-and-universities/research/textbooks.
4. Ethan Senack, *Fixing the Broken Textbook Market: How Students Respond to High Textbook Costs and Demand Alternatives*, Student Public Interest Research Groups, 2014, 4, https://studentpirgs.org/2014/01/27/fixing-broken-textbook-market; Cailyn Nagle and Kaitlyn Vitez, *Fixing the Broken Textbook Market: The Second Edition of a Report by U.S. PIRG Education Fund and the Student PIRGs*, Student Public Interest Research Groups, June 8, 2020, 2, https://studentpirgs.org/2020/06/08/fixing-the-broken-textbook-market.
5. Jacob J. Jenkins, Luis A. Sánchez, Megan AK Schraedley, Jaime Hannans, Nitzan Navick, and Jade Young, "Textbook Broke: Textbook Affordability as a Social Justice Issue," *Journal of Interactive Media in Education* 1, no. 3 (2020): 1; Salem, "Open Pathways to Student Success," 35.
6. Jenkins et al., "Textbook Broke," 5; Nicholas B. Colvard, C. Edward Watson, and Hyojin Park, "The Impact of Open Educational Resources on Various Student Success Metrics," *International Journal of Teaching and Learning in Higher Education* 30, no. 2 (2018): 262–76.
7. Vincent Tinto, "Research and Practice of Student Retention: What Next?" *Journal of College Student Retention: Research, Theory & Practice* 8, no. 1 (2006): 1–19.
8. Emily Cataldi, Christopher T. Bennett, and Xianglei Chen, "First-Generation Students: College Access, Persistence, and Postbachelor's Outcomes," National Center for Education Statistics, 2018, https://nces.ed.gov/pubsearch/pubsinfo.asp?pubid=2018421.
9. Terrie Ross, Grace Kena, Amy Rathbun, Angelina KewalRamani, Jijun Zhang, Paul Kristapovich, and Eileen Manning, "Higher Education: Gaps in Access and Persistence Study," National Center for Education Statistics, 2012, xii, https://vtechworks.lib.vt.edu/handle/10919/100555.
10. Steven Bell, "Start a Textbook Revolution, Part Two: Librarians Lead the Way with Open Educational Resources," *Library Issues: Briefings for Faculty and Administrators* 35, no. 5 (2015), http://hdl.handle.net/20.500.12613/151.

11. John H. Pollitz, Anne Christie, and Cheryl Middleton, "Management of Library Course Reserves and the Textbook Affordability Crisis," *Journal of Access Services* 6, no. 4 (2009): 459–84; Osman Celik and Roxanne Peck, "If You Expand, They Will Come: Textbook Affordability through Expansion of Course Reserves: The Case of UCLA Library's Course Reserves via Strategic Partnership with the Campus Independent Bookstore," *Technical Services Quarterly* 33, no. 3 (2016): 268–78; Diane Sotak, Jane G. Scott, and Tillia R. Griffin, "Affordable Education with a Little Help from the Library," *Reference Services Review* 48, no. 3 (2020): 457–71.

12. Charles Lyons and Dean Hendrix, "Textbook Affordability: Is There a Role for the Library?" *The Serials Librarian* 66, no. 1-4 (2014): 262–67; Steve Rokusek and Rachel Cooke, "Will Library E-Books Help Solve the Textbook Affordability Issue? Using Textbook Adoption Lists to Target Collection Development," *The Reference Librarian* 60, no. 3 (2019): 169–81.

13. Bell, "Start a Textbook Revolution."

14. Colvard et al., "Impact of Open Educational Resources."

15. Lily Todorinova and Zara T. Wilkinson, "Closing the Loop: Students, Academic Libraries, and Textbook Affordability," *Journal of Academic Librarianship* 45, no. 3 (2019): 268–77.

16. Lily Todorinova and Zara T. Wilkinson, "Incentivizing Faculty for Open Educational Resources (OER) Adoption and Open Textbook Authoring," *Journal of Academic Librarianship* 46, no. 6 (2020): 1–9.

17. Matt Badessa, "Open and Affordable Textbooks Program Reduces Textbook Costs for Students," *Rutgers Today*, August 2, 2020, www.rutgers.edu/news/open-and-affordable-textbooks-program-reduces-textbook-costs-students; Joanne Chung, "Rutgers Faculty Discuss Program to Reduce Textbook Costs," The Daily Targum, September 10, 2020, https://dailytargum.com/article/2020/09/rutgers-faculty-discuss-program-to-reduce-textbook-costs.

18. John Lai and Nicole O. Widmar, "Revisiting the Digital Divide in the COVID-19 Era," *Applied Economic Perspectives and Policy* 43, no. 1 (2021): 458–64; Gerardo E. De los Santos and Wynn Rosser, "COVID-19 Shines a Spotlight on the Digital Divide," *Change: The Magazine of Higher Learning* 53, no. 1 (2020): 22–25; Shanna S. Jaggars, Benjamin A. Motz, Marcos D. Rivera, Andrew Heckler, Joshua D. Quick, Elizabeth A. Hance, and Caroline Karwisch, "The Digital Divide among College Students: Lessons Learned from the COVID-19 Emergency Transition, Policy Report," Midwestern Higher Education Compact, 2021, https://eric.ed.gov/?id=ED611284.

19. Amy Gonzales, "The Contemporary US Digital Divide: From Initial Access to Technology Maintenance," *Information, Communication & Society* 19, no. 2 (2021): 234–48; Amy Gonzales, Jessica McCrory Calarco, and Teresa Lynch, "Technology Problems and Student Achievement Gaps: A Validation and

Extension of the Technology Maintenance Construct," *Communication Research* 47, no. 5 (2020): 750–70.
20. "Internet/Broadband Fact Sheet," Pew Research Center, 2021, www.pewresearch.org/internet/fact-sheet/internet-broadband.
21. Gonzalez et al., "Technology Problems," 759.
22. Jaggars et al., "The Digital Divide," 5.
23. Sara Goldrick-Rab, Vanessa Coca, Gregory Kienzl, Carrie R. Welton, Sonja Dahl, and Sarah Magnelia, "#RealCollege during the Pandemic: New Evidence on Basic Needs Insecurity and Student Well-Being," The Hope Center, 16, https://hope4college.com/realcollege-during-the-pandemic; Barbara Means and Julie Neisler, "Teaching and Learning in the Time of COVID: The Student Perspective," *Online Learning* 25, no. 1 (2021): 8–27.
24. Goldrick-Rab et al., "#RealCollege during the Pandemic," 16.
25. Nelson Schwartz, "'Nowhere to Hide' as Unemployment Permeates the Economy," *New York Times*, April 16, 2021, www.nytimes.com/2020/04/16/business/economy/unemployment-numbers-coronavirus.html.
26. Hansi Wang, "About Half of U.S. Homes Lost Wages during Pandemic, Census Bureau Finds," NPR, May 20, 2020, www.npr.org/sections/coronavirus-live-updates/2020/05/20/858908905/about-half-of-u-s-homes-lost-wages-during-pandemic-census-bureau-finds.
27. Rakesh Kochhar and Bennett Jesse, "U.S. Labor Market Inches Back from the COVID-19 Shock, but Recovery Is Far from Complete," Pew Research Center, 2021, www.pewresearch.org/fact-tank/2021/04/14/u-s-labor-market-inches-back-from-the-covid-19-shock-but-recovery-is-far-from-complete.
28. Goldrick-Rab et al., "#RealCollege during the Pandemic," 7.
29. Goldrick-Rab et al., "#RealCollege during the Pandemic," 14.
30. Rakesh Kochhar, "Hispanic Women, Immigrants, Young Adults, Those with Less Education Hit Hardest by COVID-19 Job Losses," Pew Research Center, 2020, www.pewresearch.org/fact-tank/2020/06/09/hispanic-women-immigrants-young-adults-those-with-less-education-hit-hardest-by-covid-19-job-losses.
31. Goldrick-Rab et al., "#RealCollege during the Pandemic," 7.
32. Goldrick-Rab et al., "#RealCollege during the Pandemic," 11–12.
33. Juliana Horowitz, Anna Brown, and Minkin Rachel, "A Year into the Pandemic, Long-Term Financial Impact Weighs Heavily on Many Americans," Pew Research Center, 2021, www.pewresearch.org/social-trends/2021/03/05/a-year-into-the-pandemic-long-term-financial-impact-weighs-heavily-on-many-americans/.
34. Michal Grinstein-Weiss, Dana C. Perantie, Samuel H. Taylor, Shenyang Guo, and Ramesh Raghavan, "Racial Disparities in Education Debt Burden among

Low- and Moderate-Income Households," *Children and Youth Services Review* 65 (2016): 166–74; Monnica Chan, Jihye Kwon, David J. Nguyen, Katherine M. Saunders, Nilkamal Shah, and Katie N. Smith, "Indebted Over Time: Racial Differences in Student Borrowing," *Educational Researcher* 48, no. 8 (2019): 558–63.

35. Min Zhan and Michael Sherraden, "Assets and Liabilities, Race/Ethnicity, and Children's College Education," *Children and Youth Services Review* 33, no. 11 (2011): 2168–75; Min Zhan and Deirdre Lanesskog, "The Impact of Family Assets and Debt on College Graduation," *Children and Youth Services Review* 43 (2014): 67–74.

36. Nicole Johnson, George Veletsianos, and Jeff Seaman, "US Faculty and Administrators' Experiences and Approaches in the Early Weeks of the COVID-19 Pandemic," *Online Learning* 24, no. 2 (2020): 6–21.

37. Quoted in Badessa, "Open and Affordable Textbooks Program."

38. Sandro Galea and Salma M. Abdalla, "COVID-19 Pandemic, Unemployment, and Civil Unrest: Underlying Deep Racial and Socioeconomic Divides," *JAMA* 324, no. 3 (2020): 227–28.

39. Abbey R. Masonbrink and Emily Hurley, "Advocating for Children during the COVID-19 School Closures," *Pediatrics* 146, no. 3 (2020).

JONATHAN ROY WILSON

14

Bridging the Digital Divide in Appalachia

Lending Technology with a Personal Librarian

Recent events associated with COVID-19 caused East Tennessee State University (ETSU) to assess and evaluate how to serve its students and their needs. COVID-19 magnified the need for technology and internet access for the university's underserved populations and the associated financial needs of college students. Locally based research indicated that the need for internet access in the surrounding communities was much greater than initially thought.[1] ETSU responded to the technology needs by forming a partnership between the departments of the Dean of Students, Student Life and Enrollment, Sherrod Library, and Information and Technology Services (ITS) in order to implement a plan to assist this underserved population.

Background

On March 16, 2020, due to COVID-19 concerns and mandates, ETSU canceled in-person instruction, and more than 5,600 on ground-only students became instant online learners. Along with instruction, all student support services moved online. This unprecedented action took place in a region where many homes lack internet or computer access. Libraries and computer labs were shuttered. ETSU scrambled to get resources for students, including loaner laptops and emergency grants for students to pay for rent, food, and internet access. The needs far outstripped ETSU's ability to respond.

In 2019, ETSU's total student enrollment of 14,885 included 10,132 (68 percent) from counties in the south central subregion of Appalachia. Under normal circumstances, the financial needs of the students from this area is great, making it difficult for many to pursue and complete a college degree.[2] ETSU had 5,111 students who were Pell Grant recipients, and the Appalachian Regional Commission (ARC) has documented the weak county economic status and college completion rates for the area.[3]

"Among the one-third of Tennesseans who live in rural communities, nearly one in four (23.2%) live in areas where broadband internet service is not available. Even where broadband is available, a quarter of all households and nearly half (49.6%) of the poorest Tennesseans (<$20,000 annual income) do not have a broadband subscription."[4] "Even with 193 internet providers operational in Tennessee, 548,000 people only have access to one provider and 274,000 people have no providers offering internet services at their place of residence."[5]

The university's instructors and librarians reported that students were completing online coursework, conducting library research, and writing essays using just their smartphones. ETSU boosted the Wi-Fi signal across campus so that students could access the internet from their cars. Up to fifty students at a time were parked on campus, working online. These were the fortunate students who possessed some kind of Wi-Fi device and the means to travel to and from campus; those without devices and means needed additional help. ETSU went from a residential to a commuter to a drive-in campus.

At the onset of the move to completely online classes in the spring of 2020, ETSU's Applied Social Research Lab administered a 33-question survey asking students about the availability of internet access and the technology needed for online learning. The first survey was sent to 13,171 students and 1,172 responded. The survey was re-sent and garnered an additional 1,090 responses. About 12 percent (419) of the respondents reported having no access to a computer, and over 20 percent (566) had no access to the internet.[6] Students from disadvantaged backgrounds were hit even harder: the TRiO program, which supports students from disadvantaged backgrounds, reported that 44 percent of the program's students lacked learning technologies in their home.

The University's Response

In the spring of 2020, ETSU's libraries initiated a two-year, campus-wide collaboration to address the digital divide that keeps many students from disadvantaged backgrounds from fully participating in online learning. A seven-member team, consisting of the deans of the Sherrod and medical libraries, the dean of students, a librarian, a library staff member, and representatives from ITS and Student Life and Enrollment, developed operational and service models for cooperation between many different units across campus: libraries, technology, student success, and others. Over the course of the program, the university integrated online service models and provided students with the technologies they needed. The program also provided students with individualized support using the "personal librarian" (PL) model to assist them with technology and online service questions and problems.

The Lending Technology & Personal Librarian Program began in a limited capacity in the spring 2020 semester by providing laptops and internet hotspots to low-income, minority, and veteran students who lacked the technology required for online learning as well as student services, which were only available online. In the fall semester 2020 and into spring semester 2021, the program expanded the number of laptops and internet hotspots available to selected students. The participants came from two student support programs—the federal TRiO program and Summer Bridge Plus—and from the general student population identified as at-risk regarding access to technology. Students living in homes lacking computers or internet could share the benefits of the technology with members of their households, thus supporting the career, educational, and information needs of the entire household.

A team of eight colleagues, six from the original team that developed the operational and service models along with an additional representative from ITS and the technology director of the library, conducted research on practices at other universities and applied for an IMLS CARES Act grant to fund laptops and hotspots.

Their research found that other colleges and universities across the nation face the same issue of lack of technology for underserved students. The financial barriers that prevent students from having personal technology to complete their academic work is not limited to any particular geographic region. For example, Louisiana State University used CARES Act funding to purchase equipment so that students would have the proper equipment to check out from the library for the semester at no cost. Most universities had to implement a plan quickly before the students started falling behind and poorly completing their course work due to digital poverty.

Many other universities are trying to remedy students' financial barriers because a lack of barriers not only helps the students academically, but also improves colleges' success and retention rates. With current stagnant wages and the growing gap of income equality, many students are struggling with financial demands. With rising tuition and textbooks costs, the expenses of higher education have become proportionally much harder for people with financial issues.

Although our library was not one of the 68 out of 1,701 applicants chosen to receive the IMLS grant funds, the team's research and organization managed to lay the groundwork for a successful program. Two members of the grant team stepped down and two people from the original team returned to accept the challenge of implementing the Lending Technology Program.

Implementation of the Lending Technology & Personal Librarian Program

The university decided that because the student need was so great, it would self-fund the project with the CARES Act monies that the campus received. ETSU committed the funds in July 2020. The university received funding totaling close to $300,000 over five months, enabling it to purchase 221 laptops, 200 hotspots, and protective cases and other supplies.

In 2020 alone, ETSU spent a total of $287,324 for equipment to enable students to navigate the online learning environment (see table 14.1). The total cost did not include the staff and faculty time that was contributed to the implementation of the program.

ETSU's ITS staff imaged and programmed the computers for the students' needs, and the library staff cataloged and barcoded them for checkout. Sherrod Library staff also developed promotional material to accompany the items when they were checked out.

TABLE 14.1
Technology funded by CARES Act

July 2020	ETSU's Information Technology Service's CARES funds	200 Verizon wireless hotspots at $426 each	$85,200 per year
		25 Dell Latitude 3400 laptops	$17,029
August 2020	Information Technology Services (ITS) CARES funds	66 Dell Latitude 7400/3410 laptops	$54,060
November 2020	University provides additional CARES Act funding to project	130 Dell Latitude 5410 laptops	$128,310
		Supplies and protective cases	$2,725
Total			**$287,324**

Initial promotion of the lending program proceeded slowly during the fall semester 2020. The first promotions started with the dean of students reaching out to different entities on campus, such as the academic advisors and other departments, through the campus-wide Academic Council and other departmental meetings. The dean of students also placed a form on their web page where students could apply for financial services and the lending technology. Students could then arrange to pick up the technology in person, at curbside, or through priority mail for distant students. In November 2020, the program's promotion was increased by involving Student Life and Enrollment and the Center for Academic Achievement. In the spring semester of 2021, the program was also advertised on the Sherrod Library's web page,[7] at the Medical Library (specifically targeting the rural-remote medical students), in the *Sherrod Library Newsletter,* and in an article printed in the student newspaper, *The East Tennessean*.[8] The directors of the off-campus sites in Kingsport and Sevierville were also notified and encouraged to promote the program.

Impact of the Lending Technology Program

In the fall of 2020, 138 students received laptops or hotspots in the program. In that same semester a survey was sent to the participants, and 29 completed it. When asked the question "Did having the equipment help you complete your courses?" 27 responded that it helped them very much, one said somewhat, and one responded not much.

In response to the question, "How did having the equipment help? Check all that apply," 22 indicated better (faster and more stable) internet access, as well as saving time. Twenty-one also indicated that they saved money.

On the survey, students also had the opportunity to comment on the program. Their comments emphasized the financial and academic benefits of the program.

- "Saved time. Having a very good and fast laptop computer to complete my numerous assignments and end-of-term projects was such a huge help that aided my fall term success. It saved me more than just time (to complete tasks), it also saved me the stress of having to visit (even on days not very comfortable doing so) my department's computer lab to get tasks done."
- "It was easy getting resources since the Librarian was always on standby to offer help when needed."
- "Better internet access—faster, more stable, saved money, saved time, less stress."
- "I felt more relaxed since I had the necessary resources, and I was able to come out with better grades."
- "Amazing, I simply would not have been able to do college online if it weren't for the hot spots. I have no reliable internet source in my area and would have had to just up and move or live with a friend if it weren't for the hotspots."[9]

Figure 14.1 shows the 2020 fall semester student participants by major. In the fall semester, checkouts were noticeably large among the nursing and

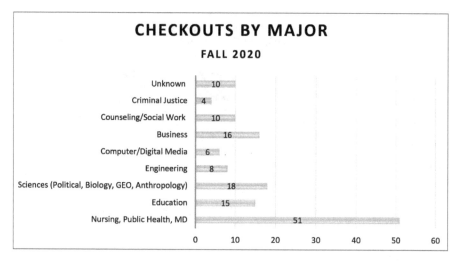

FIGURE 14.1
Checkout of laptops and/or hotspots by student major, fall 2020

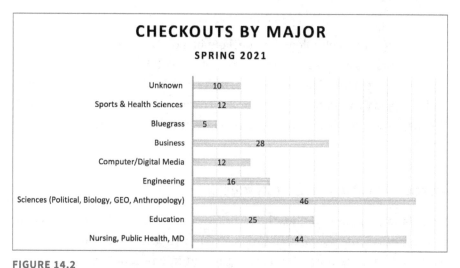

FIGURE 14.2
Checkout of laptops and/or hotspots by student major, spring 2021

public health students. Among the reasons for this were that the students in that subject area are required to do clinical rotations in rural areas, and they had to have internet access and the proper equipment. Also, some of the programs that they use require the proper equipment in order to work. Another large group by major that checked out equipment was the science majors, with a substantial growth in the spring 2021 semester, when the

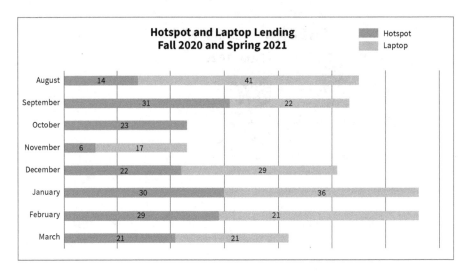

FIGURE 14.3
Hotspot and laptop lending by month, 2020–2021

availability of the technology for checkout had become better known among the students (figure 14.2). In the spring of 2021, 198 students received laptops and/or hotspots. Figure 14.3 shows the number of checkouts of laptops and hotspots by month from August 2020 through March 2021. As expected, the majority of students checked out the equipment at the beginning of the semester.

Personal Librarian Services

Part of the program—besides the technology—which has played a key factor in its success is the personal librarian, or PL. The personal librarian contacts each student once they have been approved to check out equipment, and provides a variety of services for the students, including acting as a liaison to ETSU resources such as Bucky's Food Pantry, the University Health Clinic, the Counseling Center, Disability Services, and tutoring services. The PL reaches out to the students on a weekly basis through e-mail messages that offer information about library workshops, available resources on campus, and important dates such as registration and events that are happening on or around campus. Additionally, the PL offers one-on-one meetings for research needs such as finding peer-reviewed scholarly articles and providing citation help. The PL also helps students troubleshoot technical and equipment issues, and assists students with capstone and thesis projects.

As the point of contact for students in the program, the PL also developed an assessment to determine which services are needed more than others, prioritizing what the students actually need in order to better understand how to serve those with financial needs.

Discussion

Over the past two semesters, the Lending Technology Program has served a large variety of students, including both traditional and nontraditional ones. The students' needs are as varied as the students themselves. The primary factor that the program has identified is the financial issues affecting proper equipment and/or internet access. Most of the students that the program serves are living from paycheck to paycheck, and having stable access to appropriate, working equipment reduces a major stressor so that they can successfully complete their academic requirements and continue their education.

Other reasons for students' participation in the program include technical issues or broken personal equipment, in which case the student needs a laptop for a week or two until they can afford to fix their device. Some students who are going home for the weekend or for an extended time period don't have internet access at home. Others are traveling for sporting or other university events. A few participants had family emergencies and needed the technology until the situation was resolved. Other students have had to quarantine and needed the technology to stay enrolled in classes.

As ETSU moved forward into the fall 2021 semester and classes began transitioning back to an on-site format, the program's goal has been expanded to target existing and potential students with financial needs, and provide PLs to all first-year and transfer students. The COVID-19 shutdown of the physical campus highlighted the tremendous need for financial support of students who lack hardware or sustainable internet access. Even though the university was aware of the socioeconomic makeup of the service area, the magnitude of the digital divide was only truly revealed by the pandemic.

In response, ETSU decided to be more involved in implementing solutions to strengthen student success, retention, and enrollment. The implementation team is exploring methods to promote and expand the program and is reviewing and planning for sustainability, especially the annual costs for hotspots and for future laptop replacement when their four-year warranty expires.

NOTES

1. East Tennessee State University, Applied Social Research Lab, "Student Survey," Johnson City, April–May 2020.
2. East Tennessee State University, "East Tennessee State University Fact Book," Johnson City, 2019, www.etsu.edu/opa/fact/factbooks.aspx.
3. Kelvin Pollard and Linda A. Jacobsen, "The Appalachian Region: A Data Overview from the 2014–2018 American Community Survey Chartbook," Appalachian Regional Commission, June 2020, 53–79, www.arc.gov/wp-content/uploads/2020/08/DataOverviewfrom2014to2018ACS.pdf.
4. Think Tennessee, Center for Rural Strategies, "State of Our State Policy Brief: Broadband Internet," 1, www.thinktennessee.org/wp-content/uploads/2020/11/state-of-our-state-policy-review-brief_-broadband-internet_final.pdf.
5. Cooper Tyler, "Internet Access in Tennessee: Stats & Figures," BroadbandNow, March 10, 2021, https://broadbandnow.com/Tennessee.
6. Applied Social Research Lab, "Student Survey."
7. East Tennessee State University, Sherrod Library web page, https://libraries.etsu.edu/use/computers/lendingtech/home.
8. Nicholas Crockett, "Lending Technology Program Aims to Get Students Online," *The East Tennessean*, March 8, 2021, https://easttennessean.com/2021/03/08/lending-technology-program-aims-to-get-students-online.
9. Jonathan Wilson and Celia Szarejko, "Sherrod Library Technology Lending/Personal Librarian Service Feedback Survey," East Tennessee State University, December 2020.

SHANNON L. DEW, GRETCHEN MITCHELL, AND SUSAN B. MYTHEN

Laptops for Students
An Academic and Public Library Partnership

In March 2020, Florida State College at Jacksonville (FSCJ) moved all classes to a virtual environment and closed campus buildings in response to the COVID-19 pandemic. Courses originally meeting in face-to-face or hybrid modalities transitioned to "live online," with weekly virtual class meetings. This move to remote learning left many FSCJ students without regular access to their courses. To offer immediate relief, the college reopened two campus libraries for very limited services, allowing students to use computer labs for their coursework. This met the needs of some students, but those without transportation or who had work or family responsibilities during the libraries' limited hours of operation struggled to complete assignments and attend virtual class meetings.

FSCJ quickly responded by requesting federal CARES Act funding to help students with educational financial support, and received $7.25 million on May 6, 2020. A portion of this funding was distributed directly to students. Funding to the college provided for a number of student support programs, such as providing additional technology to students in the form of laptops and webcams to aid in the completion of online coursework. A total of 400 student laptops were purchased through CARES Act funding.

Background

Florida State College at Jacksonville is an open-access, multi-campus state college with seven libraries serving approximately 44,000 students. FSCJ serves students in Duval and Nassau counties in northeast Florida. Jacksonville is the largest city in the continental United States by area, and the population of the city and its surrounding communities is approximately 1.6 million. The FSCJ service area includes urban, suburban, and rural areas. Approximately 66 percent of FSCJ students receive financial aid.

The digital divide presents a serious obstacle to access for many Jacksonville residents, and as education and services moved fully online in 2020 the divide became even more apparent. According to the Pew Research Center,[1] 44 percent of U.S. households with incomes under $30,000 a year are without broadband, and 46 percent are without a computer. In lower-income households, individuals are more likely to rely on smartphones for tasks that are better suited to a computer, including homework.[2] In the city of Jacksonville, nearly 10 percent of households have no computer.[3]

Removing barriers to information is central to the mission of libraries. Libraries are often called upon to fill the information access gap in the communities they serve by offering ways for patrons to borrow digital devices, access computer labs, and obtain technology training.[4] In academic libraries, this often includes laptop lending. These laptop-lending programs typically allow students to use the laptops for short-term checkout periods (usually two hours) either in the library or elsewhere on campus, and stock between 20 and 100 laptops in their inventory.[5] Dunnington and Simpson discussed the lending program at the Southeastern Louisiana University Library, including its time limitations, checkout procedures, and security issues. They found that students were interested in longer checkout periods and faster-running devices.[6] Wang and Arlain reported on the Ryerson University Library's laptop loan program and its implementation of a self-checkout system. They emphasized the importance of approaching laptop-lending projects as a reflection of the institution's larger goals.[7] Each of these studies noted a need for better IT support of student laptop lending.

At universities and residential colleges, these library lending programs are often used by students on campus who have a PC or laptop but don't want to carry it around with them.[8] In a review of the literature, only one two-year college, Georgia Piedmont Technical College, had published information on laptop lending. In that 2015 study, Wilmoth found that "students overwhelmingly stated that of all mobile devices, laptops were the most important to facilitate their success in school."[9]

Phase 1: The College Laptop-Lending Program

FSCJ implemented a process to distribute 400 laptops to students who were impacted by the transition to remote learning due to COVID-19 and who qualified based on several federal criteria. These students had

- completed the 2019/2020 FASFA (Free Application for Federal Student Aid);
- enrolled in a degree or certificate program, meeting federal standards for satisfactory academic progress;
- enrolled in six of more semester credit hours; and
- had an expected family contribution on the FASFA application indicating some unmet financial need (at least $600 to receive a laptop).

The initial goal was to distribute a laptop as a financial aid award to each student who met the criteria. While the student would not be charged for the device, the amount would be taken from their overall unmet financial need. This had some students apprehensive about receiving the laptops. Additionally, many students have financial need yet do not meet the strict federal criteria. Therefore, FSCJ shifted 100 of the laptops to the library's long-term equipment lending program, and the library established policies and procedures to loan these 100 laptops and distribute the remaining 300 as financial aid awards.

Marketing to Students and Faculty

FSCJ's Marketing and Communications Office distributed an e-mail to all FSCJ students sharing information on how to receive a laptop for their online coursework. A "Survey of Student Readiness in Online Learning" was included in the e-mail for students to complete, and more than 700 students responded indicating interest in the program. From this initial e-blast, only 100 of them were identified as meeting the eligibility criteria for an award. For the students who did not meet the eligibility requirements, the lending program filled the gap and provided equal access to the equipment for any enrolled FSCJ student.

The "Survey of Student Readiness in Online Learning" was also added to a college LibGuide so as to enable additional students to request technology throughout the year. The LibGuide was designed as an information hub for students and faculty, who could see the equipment available to students and receive guidance on how to obtain the equipment. Marketing to faculty and students continued throughout the fall 2020 and spring 2021 semesters. The survey was removed from the site at the end of the initial program in April 2021.

Initial Circulation Data

All laptops purchased with federal CARES Act funds were required to be distributed to students through an award or lending program by the end of April 2021. As of April 19, 2021, 23 of the 300 computers designated as financial awards had not been collected, so the library moved them to the lending program (for distribution data, see figure 15.1).

The technology lending program data was collected from circulation records and was entered onto a spreadsheet for grant reporting. November

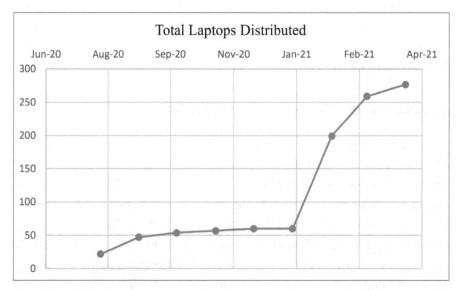

FIGURE 15.1
Laptop award program data: August 2020–April 2021

TABLE 15.1
Lending program circulation data: October 2020–March 2021

	Loans	Renewal	Returns
October 2020	77	1	1
November 2020	27	0	4
December 2020	5	10	67
January 2021	80	0	19
February 2021	16	0	18
March 2021	5	0	1
TOTAL	**210**	**11**	**110**

2020 was the second month the laptops were available for borrowing, and by the end of that month, all 100 laptops had been loaned. In December the library allowed students to renew, provided they showed proof of enrollment and payment for the spring 2021 term. By the second month of that term, all 100 laptops had been borrowed. As soon as one was returned, it would be checked out almost immediately by another student.

The laptops on loan to students were due at the end of the semester. At the end of the fall semester, seven laptops had not been returned, and due to the high demand and cost of the laptops, the students' accounts were charged. This was a difficult decision, as the students had already indicated financial hardship.

At the end of the fall and spring semesters, students were e-mailed a survey asking about their satisfaction with the technology lending and award programs and how these had impacted their coursework at FSCJ. Most students were very satisfied with the programs and shared positive responses about their experiences. As one student response noted, "I did not own a laptop, could not afford a laptop, so when everything went online due to the pandemic, I was extremely worried. When I was told about the lending program I jumped on the opportunity, and the entire process was seamless. Everyone who helped along the process was wonderful as well. This program allowed me to continue my studies when I never would have been able to prior."

Phase 2: College and Public Library Partnership

The college and its foundation were looking for ways to reach students who were having difficulty traveling to the FSCJ's Deerwood Center, where the laptops were being distributed. To meet the technology needs of these students, representatives of the college (FSCJ) and the Florida State College of Jacksonville Foundation (FSCJF) reached out to the Jacksonville Public Library (JPL) about a collaborative effort to make computers more accessible to these students. The public library, with its twenty-one locations covering the 874 square miles of Jacksonville, made an ideal partner (see figure 15.2). For the JPL, it was an appealing opportunity to collaborate with FSCJ and a chance to experiment with device lending.

The FSCJ, FSCJF, and the JPL considered all possible gifting options and the various requirements and ramifications of each within the confines of their

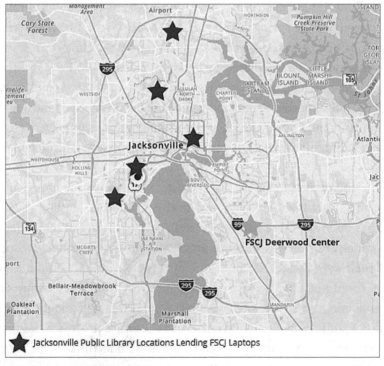

FIGURE 15.2
Map of FSCJ laptop-lending locations

various organizational regulations. The FSCJ Foundation donated twenty-five laptop computers in order to expand the college's lending program to the public library. The laptops were for the exclusive use of FSCJ students through designated public library sites. Donors to the FSCJF provided funding for the project, and the JPL's Board of Library Trustees formally accepted the gift. The agreement between the organizations included the following conditions:

- The computers will be for the exclusive use of current, validated FSCJ students (enrolled in at least one class) who visit designated public library sites.
- The public library will develop specific (local) governance, maintenance, oversight, and auditing mechanisms related to the lending of the computers.
- The pilot project's duration will be determined by mutual agreement of the administrations of the FSCJ and the library, and its scope, timeline, and methods of determining success will be established during the pilot project.
- Upon receipt, the technology devices will be owned by the library, and as such the library will have no responsibility or obligation to repair or replace any of the devices. Should it decide to do so, all maintenance will follow the library's existing maintenance and servicing procedures.
- The devices will be loaned to students for the duration of an entire term according to FSCJ's academic calendar, and upon return they will be repurposed, reimaged, or cleaned by the library for recirculation during the next following term.

Because of educational privacy laws (FERPA), FSCJ's Marketing and Communications Office, rather than the JPL, sent targeted e-mails to students containing a link to the JPL's web page about the program; the page describes the program and includes a link to the laptop catalog record and resources of interest to college students.[10] Doing this not only put content on the JPL's website but also allowed the e-mail newsletter sent by the Marketing and Communications Office to stay short and to the point. Direct marketing to students was more effective for the JPL, since device-lending programs for the general public are not available.

The JPL developed an implementation plan while negotiations on the donation agreement were being finalized. This plan covered finalizing locations, planning equipment setup and maintenance, updating circulation policies and creating procedures, and mapping communications. To expedite the process and make laptops available as quickly as possible, the project team focused on making choices that kept requirements simple. The JPL modeled the student borrowing agreement after the one used by the FSCJ. It outlines the rules of use, and after signing, students receive a copy.

Placement of the twenty-five laptops was based on geography and public transportation routes. The FSCJ representatives suggested circulating them from libraries located in the north and west sections of the city. The FSCJ laptop-lending program, located in southeast Jacksonville, was not as accessible for students without convenient transportation. The JPL opted to place five laptops at each of the four identified branches in the north and west areas of town as well as five laptops at the Main Library, centrally located downtown. All five locations are on public transportation routes.

The project team worked with the Board of Library Trustees to revise the circulation policy to include all relevant lending information, including the exclusive use by FSCJ students.[11] It required that the students be enrolled in the current semester and have a valid Jacksonville Public Library card. Additionally, the team drafted operational procedures and worked with managers of the five locations to finalize them. The procedures provided details on inventory requirements, the checkout process, return process, damaged device process, and non-return process. Per operational procedure, the laptop and charger are checked out to the student with the due date reflecting the last day of the semester.

External communication was managed by JPL's Community Relations and Marketing, with the project team providing the information. Internal communication and training were managed by the project team. The training of branch staff on changes in circulation policy and on the operational procedures was completed by the five managers with project team members. An informational all-staff e-mail was sent before going live. The e-mail provided links to the laptop landing page on the JPL website and links to all related documentation located on the internal staff site.

Discussion and Analysis

The JPL-FSCJ laptop project went live on February 17, 2021. In the first month, 13 of the 25 laptops were borrowed and by October, 24 of the 25 had been loaned. Feedback on the project so far is anecdotal. Staff involved in checking out the laptops reported that some students volunteered that they had previously shared computers with family members and were excited to have an exclusive device. To increase use in the next semester, the JPL is working with FSCJ on continued direct marketing to students and faculty. The library is also moving several of the laptops from two of the low-use branches to another branch based on the available use data.

At FSCJ, the lending program proved more popular than the award program. Many students were denied an award laptop for not carrying six credits, not being enrolled in a degree program (such as students in adult education and ESOL programs), or not qualifying for federal financial aid for other reasons. Even though the library contacted over 400 eligible students to inform them of the program and that a laptop was available for them, students were hesitant about the financial aid aspect of the program and preferred to borrow a device.

FSCJ plans to continue the equipment-lending program and expand the program to four additional library locations. However, there have been challenges with this program. Some students were reluctant to return their laptop after multiple attempts to contact them. As of October 2021, approximately a year after the program began, 27 laptops were not returned to the library and set to a lost status. This is roughly a $16,200 loss. The library is exploring computer locking programs such as Windows' "Find My Device" for future use, to allow staff to locate and lock any device not returned to the library.

Another challenge the FSCJ library encountered was getting technical support. The IT department helped with the initial setup and reimage process, but was not able to assist with any damage or technical support beyond that, due to limited staff in their department. The public library also acknowledged limited technical support for the program.

Conclusion

For any school or library with a focus on digital equity, laptop-lending programs are an important component. Providing students with long-term laptop circulation or a technology award can give our most vulnerable students access to courseware and digital materials at a time and location that meets their needs. Students indicated their overwhelming support for this program and reported that it was a major influence on their decision to continue in school. This program also demonstrated the effectiveness of a public-academic library partnership in meeting the needs of the community's most vulnerable students. Both libraries look forward to future opportunities for partnership.

NOTES

1. "Digital Divide Persists Even as Lower-Income Americans Make Gains in Tech Adoption," *Pew Research Center* (blog), www.pewresearch.org/fact-tank/2019/05/07/digital-divide-persists-even-as-lower-income-americans-make-gains-in-tech-adoption.
2. "U.S. Census Bureau QuickFacts: Jacksonville City, Florida," U.S. Census Bureau, www.census.gov/quickfacts/jacksonvillecityflorida.
3. "U.S. Census Bureau QuickFacts."
4. David Lee King, "Library Technology Reports," *Library Technology Reports* 57, no. 2 (March 2, 2021): 5–36.
5. Weina Wang et al., "From a Knowledge Container to a Mobile Learning Platform: What RULA Learned from the Laptop Lending Program," *Journal of Access Services* 11, no. 4 (October 2014): 255–81, https://doi.org/10.1080/15367967.2014.945118; Weina Wang and Mandissa Arlain, "Laptops to Go," *Computers in Libraries* 34, no. 3 (April 2014): 12–16; Angela Dunnington and Bethany Simpson, "Lessons Learned in Laptop Lending: The Southeastern Louisiana University Experience," *Louisiana Libraries* 75, no. 4 (Spring 2013): 14–18.
6. Dunnington and Simpson, "Lessons Learned in Laptop Lending."
7. Wang and Arlain, "Laptops to Go."
8. Wang et al., "From a Knowledge Container to a Mobile Learning Platform."

9. Wendy S. Wilmoth, "Circulating Laptops in a Two-Year Academic Library: A Formative Assessment," *Georgia Library Quarterly* 52, no. 4 (Fall 2015): 1–11.
10. "FSCJ Laptop Borrowing," Jacksonville Public Library, February 8, 2021, https://jaxpubliclibrary.org/services/fscj-laptop-borrowing.
11. "Circulation Policy," Jacksonville Public Library, September 27, 2016, https://jaxpubliclibrary.org/about/policies/circulation-policy.

PAIZHA STOOTHOFF

16

Paid Positions for Students
A Win-Win for Everyone Involved

In most fields, paid entry-level work opportunities are in demand, but they are unfortunately less common than mid- or senior-level positions. For undergraduate students interested in careers in libraries or museums, this predicament is amplified by internship eligibility criteria that require applicants to be enrolled in master of library and information science (MLIS) or similar degree programs.[1] This, in part, has led to a serious lack of diversity in the profession. Paid work experiences in academic libraries for nontraditional, first-generation students can be incredibly valuable not only to students, but also to librarians and to the profession as a whole. In this chapter, the author will discuss how librarians can collaborate with archivists, library staff, professors, and students to offer paid positions to undergraduate students. For the author of this chapter, collaboratively creating and implementing paid positions resulted in higher-quality, more rewarding experiences for students and librarians alike.

Background

Declining university enrollment is a persistent issue that has impacted both the humanities disciplines and library science. In 2020, university enrollment in the United States dropped by 3.6 percent from the previous year, amounting to more than 560,000 students.[2] Amidst declining enrollments, the humanities disciplines and libraries are particularly vulnerable to budget reductions and hiring freezes. These issues are particularly prevalent at universities like California State University, Los Angeles (Cal State LA), where the most common majors are in the social sciences, criminal justice, and computer science and engineering.[3] Cal State LA is a large public university in east Los Angeles that serves approximately 30,000 students annually. A majority of our students are the first in their families to go to college (58 percent are first-generation) and are from local, low-income households (62 percent are Pell Grant eligible).[4] Keeping the cost of college low and finding a job after graduation are top priorities for students. The practicality of pursuing a degree such as English and a career in librarianship is a concern for many students.

For the reasons discussed above, many academics are in a "rhetoric of crisis" about the decline of the humanities and similar disciplines.[5] One alternative approach, however, is to look carefully at curricula and programs to find ways to innovate beyond our comfort zones, by forming interdisciplinary alliances, for example.[6] At Cal State LA, the English Department and the University Library collaborate to provide paid work opportunities for undergraduate students who are majoring in English. These efforts are supported by the English Department's "Engaged English" curriculum, which was launched in 2019 to help students connect the dots between their majors and potential careers by offering internships and new courses such as archival studies, grant-writing, and narrative as therapy. Likewise, the University Library's 2019 strategic plan highlights the importance of exploring new partnerships and expanding student engagement.[7] English is a discipline that has traditionally attracted students interested in museums and libraries; however, as stated previously, professional development opportunities are typically limited to MLIS students. Together, our departments provide students with paid opportunities through which they can learn about library careers.

This chapter discusses the methods and benefits of offering paid work experiences to nontraditional, historically underserved undergraduate students in academic libraries, with a focus on positions that are integrated into departmental curricula.

Literature Review

Internships are beneficial for students' academic success as well as the development of their personal competencies. Internships have been shown to improve students' multicultural skills and cultural competence, particularly in programs where they are encouraged to think about how race and class influence their interactions with others.[8] Internships for undergraduate students have also been shown to improve students' GPAs at Hispanic-serving institutions (HSIs) and among seniors who have lower grades as freshmen.[9] The demonstrated benefit of internships for students with initially lower grades is extremely important because it indicates that the mentorship and hands-on experience are particularly valuable for underserved students who are at risk of dropping out. However, the quality of the internship experience directly correlates to the benefits derived from it. Therefore, incorporating best practices is of paramount importance for librarians who are considering designing and offering internships or other work experiences for undergraduate students.

The importance of incorporating best practices into student internships and work experiences is well-documented by the literature. One recommended approach is to use "high-impact practices," which are widely known to benefit student educational experiences.[10] Internships can be highly impactful when student interns have opportunities to identify their interests, discover connections between their majors and future careers, and practice their knowledge. Examples of high-impact practices in internships include offering effort-driven tasks that require critical and deep thinking; facilitating collaborative work that builds relationships; encouraging students to engage across differences; providing feedback formally and informally; and helping students test what they have learned by designing activities around learning outcomes rather than assigning a series of unrelated tasks.[11] These high-impact practices enable students to integrate what they have learned with real-world experience, allowing them to discover what they want (and do not want) to do. In one study, Kopp applied high-impact practices to a special collections internship program by designing a series of tracks around student learning objectives and incorporating experiential learning activities. The students reported highly positive experiences, and the program strengthened campus partnerships.[12]

While a meaningful, quality work experience is certainly a form of incentive, librarians should consider other incentives, such as academic credit, grades, and monetary compensation. Monetary compensation is valuable at universities like Cal State LA, where students have financial need and are more likely than their continuing education peers to be juggling work, school, and family commitments. Minority first-generation students are also more likely to experience deficit-model teaching, microaggressions, and hidden curricula, which decrease morale and can lead to lower graduation rates.[13] Providing paid work experiences facilitates a culture of mutual respect and appreciation, which can help reduce stress and anxiety. However, the limitations imposed by monetary compensation should be considered when designing an internship or similar position. Methods for payment and reporting for work performed can dictate the structure of the internship, especially if compensation is established at the university or department level.[14] While some payment methods, such as stipends, enable supervisors to design flexible projects and experiences, other methods, such as hourly positions paid by a grant or university administration, are more rigid. Two payment models utilized at Cal State LA are discussed below. Librarians can align the work their libraries need with students' professional experiences, while also considering the limitations that payment methods will have on their students, library, and job program.[15]

Position Design

Paid work experiences for students can be provided through student assistantships or internships. Both of these employment models were used at the University Library at Cal State LA between 2019 and 2021 and are discussed in detail below.

Student Assistants (Digitization Assistants)

In the fall of 2019, the library recruited and hired two digitization assistants within the framework of the student assistantship model to work on a grant-funded project to digitize a student-edited literary magazine called *Statement Magazine*. The grant was provided by the Cal State LA Library, which offers annual innovation grants of up to $3,000 for library staff and/or librarians. The digitization assistants worked 4 hours per week and were paid hourly at a rate of $13.00 per hour. The students documented their hours in time logs, which they reported on a biweekly basis as required by library policy.

The supervising librarians were strategic in creating the positions and recruiting students with a demonstrated interest in publishing and digitization. To create these hourly paid positions, the liaison librarian for English (the humanities librarian) and the archivist and special collections librarian collaborated to identity the need for the digitization, write a grant that budgeted for two paid positions, and design positions that incorporated learning objectives that would be valuable for English majors interested in archival studies and publishing. To recruit student assistants, the librarians conduct outreach in English 3920, "Statement and Literary Magazine Editing and Publishing." With approval from the English department chair and the Statement Magazine faculty advisor, we attended the class to talk about the opportunity with students who were interested in literary magazine publishing. The job description was also posted through the campus job website and the English Department's Facebook page. These recruitment methods resulted in a pool of more than 15 applicants, at least 5 of whom were English majors. We hired two of the English majors, one of whom was enrolled in the magazine-publishing class and one of whom was actively involved in the magazine's extracurricular activities. Both expressed interest in learning about digitization and archival science. These recruitment and hiring strategies helped the librarians to match their needs with student interests and the curriculum.

The training and onboarding of the students was relatively seamless because Cal State LA's Special Collections Department had previously created a student assistant program, and it supplied us with its existing onboarding and workflows. Group trainings provided a peer-learning environment, while individual work hours enabled the students to read and practice digitization tasks. The trainings supported students in learning and discussing concepts, such as the importance of quality scanning and metadata, before applying that knowledge by using a professional overhead scanner and creating metadata. Unfortunately, this project was put on hold in March 2020 due to COVID-19 and the closure of the library, including all in-person labor. The students were not able to resume work remotely, and due to the inflexibility of grant funds and the limited library budget, we were unable to retain the students.

Library Interns

The library internships were created with a different model and more flexible funding. Unlike the student assistant positions, which were hourly, grant-funded positions that required students to work only on the digitization project, the library internships offered a great degree of flexibility. The chair of the English Department agreed that the internships would support its relatively new "Engaged English" pathway, which includes paid internships for course credit. The English Department faculty allocate four $1,500 stipends for these internships, and the department collaborates with faculty to develop meaningful positions. For English majors interested in academic librarianship, a basic library internship is an ideal setting to learn more about the profession and to gain tangible experience.

In the spring of 2021, the library hired two library interns from the English Department. The internships were for credit and took place remotely due to COVID-19, using videoconferencing for synchronous contact and Canvas for asynchronous modules or tracks. The internship program was created using a backward design approach, whereby the librarians compiled a list of projects and asked the students to rank their top five choices from the list. During this initial phase, we also videoconferenced with students to provide an introduction to academic librarianship and answer any questions. The internship was offered by the humanities librarian and the archivist and special collections librarian due to students' expressed interests in English liaison librarianship, collection development, and archiving. In general, however, librarians can and should collaborate with each other and students to select work projects that reflect students' interests.

Based on the students' expressed interests, the librarians crafted learning outcomes and activities around the following three tracks:

1. Library instruction and research support
2. Collection development
3. Special collections and archives

In each track, overviews of key concepts were assigned before projects began, which ensured that students engaged with the concepts intellectually before moving on to practical tasks. For example, both students expressed an interest in collection development. Hence, the students watched asynchronous videos and read about collection development through Canvas, identified and added curricular areas (e.g., Latinx women's poetry) to a collection development plan, and identified five to ten books using the library's acquisition platform, GOBI. The projects for library instruction and archives varied based on the students' preferences.

Findings

Both the student assistant and internship models provided paid work experiences for undergraduate students who were interested in library and archival science. The figure below indicates the pros and cons for each type of position. The elements in the left-hand column are borrowed from Candice Dahl's internship framework, which identifies structure, projects, compensation, and documentation as the key elements present in internships.[16]

Discussion

Through collaborations within the library, with departments on campus, and with members of the community, librarians can leverage their strengths in outreach and relationship-building to identify resources and promote the value of the library through the design of tailored student positions. (Involving community organizations is an area not covered by this chapter that deserves more attention.) The author of this chapter found that paid work experiences should incorporate not only task-based activities, but also deeper learning experiences that improve students' personal competencies and other skills, such as critical thinking and information literacy. Even if positions are limited in scope, librarians can work with students to identify their interests and creatively match students to related learning experiences, such as readings and short videos, discussions, and tangible tasks. While some projects such as digitization initiatives require in-person work, librarians can also provide remote work experiences that continue to be needed by students during the COVID-19 pandemic. Many librarians have greatly improved their asynchronous and hybrid teaching skills during the pandemic and can now offer this flexible structure for undergraduate students, and librarians can advocate for funding that facilitates flexible paid work experiences for students.

FIGURE 16.1
Comparison of pros and cons of internships and student assistantships

Element	Position	Pros	Cons
Structure (i.e., the timing, number of hours worked, accountability to outcomes)	Intern	Flexibility	Can be too open-ended
	Student Assistant	Simplicity	Can be rigid
Projects (i.e., learning opportunities, tasks)	Intern	Creativity	Danger of doing too much
	Student Assistant	Focused	Redundancy of work due to limitations of grant-funded project activities
Compensation	Intern	Less paperwork; lump sum	Dependent on outside departments
	Student Assistant	Consistent paycheck	Dependent on grant or internal funds
Documentation (i.e., requirements for offering work experiences, reporting, etc.).	Intern	There may be no parameters.	Less infrastructure to support workflows or structure.
	Student Assistant	Established workflows/documentation	Can create busy work or red tape

Recommendation
Plan ahead. Clearly communicate expectations early on. Be consistent with the timing of contacts.
Build in dynamic and engaging learning opportunities to trainings and meetings.
Focus. Rather than doing everything students may express interest in, do more with less.
Dive deep into intellectual concepts that ask students to think critically and engage with one another rather than only focusing on tasks. Help students connect dots.
Understand any requirements students must meet to receive department stipends and be transparent early.
Understand procedures for student reporting and payment.
Identify any documentation requirements. Get creative with planning and collaborate with students about setting up parameters for their own internship.
Work within the parameters given. Check-in with students about their own documentation hurdles to avoid frustration or isolation.

Student internships and assistantships are also fertile ground for mentorship. In both position models described in this chapter, the librarians intentionally hired two students to enable team-based learning and collaborative projects, such as working on a collection development plan together to identify curricular areas to purchase books. Each student brought their own perspective and knowledge of English literature to the plan, which provided the librarian with an authentic setting to discuss the purpose of subject expertise in academic liaison librarianship. While librarians operated as supervisors for both positions, they were not responsible for grading the students. The student assistants were hired as part-time employees, so the connection to the English curriculum was intentional but did not require grading. For the library internship, the students enrolled in a supplementary class where they reflected on their experiences and were graded by a faculty advisor in the English Department. Through formal feedback on ungraded task logs and informal feedback via messages or virtual meetings, the students often asked questions and even took on new tasks as time allowed. The flexibility of the internship enabled the students to select areas that interested them as they went along.

Conclusion

When we interviewed candidates for the student assistant and library intern positions, several students were excited to see a library job/internship posting. In their experiences, work opportunities in libraries and archives had been rare and incredibly competitive. Librarianship is a common career pathway for English majors, but it is also a very competitive field that is lacking in diversity. Providing paid work opportunities for students at a Hispanic-serving institution introduces students to a prospective career, enabling students who might otherwise pass over librarianship due to the cost barriers of graduate school or the lack of entry-level work opportunities in the profession. Making sure that those opportunities are both meaningful and paid will further encourage students to apply for positions. Just as important, however, is the question of what librarians and libraries can do for students. Internships and other part-time work experiences are incredibly valuable for students, even if they decide against pursuing work in the profession.

The benefits include supporting students in discovering what they do and do not want, developing a network, and gaining professional experience that can have value in other fields. When they are structured with high-impact practices, paid positions for students enable undergraduate students to explore career options in libraries and can contribute to a more diversified profession.

NOTES

1. Communities: A Team-Based Engagement Framework for Student Employment in Academic Libraries," *Journal of Library Administration* 56 (2016): 251–65, https://doi.org/10.1080/01930826.2015.1121662.
2. National Student Clearinghouse Research Center, "Current Term Enrollment Estimates," 2020, https://nscresearchcenter.org/current-term-enrollment-estimates/.
3. "Cooperative Institutional Research Program (CIRP) Freshman Survey," 2020, Cal State LA, www.calstatela.edu/sites/default/files/groups/Institutional%20Research/SurveyResults/tfs_2020_powerpoint.pdf.
4. Cal State LA, Institutional Effectiveness, "Student Enrollment," spring 2021, www.calstatela.edu/InstitutionalEffectiveness/student-enrollment.
5. James F. English, *The Global Future of English Studies* (Hoboken, NJ: John Wiley & Sons, 2012), xii.
6. English, *Global Future of English Studies*.
7. "Library Strategic Plan," Cal State LA, 2019, www.calstatela.edu/sites/default/files/groups/University%20Library/Forms/2018-21libdirns.pdf.
8. Lori Simons, Lawrence Fehr, Nancy Blank, Heather Connel, Denise Georganas, David Fernandez, and Verda Peterson, "Lessons Learned from Experiential Learning: What Do Students Learn from a Practicum/Internship," *International Journal of Teaching and Learning in Higher Education* 24, no. 3, (2012): 325–34, www.isetl.org/ijtlhe/pdf/IJTLHE1315.pdf.
9. Eugene T. Parker III, Cindy Kilgo, Jessica K. Ezel Sheets, and Ernest T. Pascarella, "The Differential Effects of Internship Participation on End-of-Fourth-Year GPA by Demographic and Institutional Characteristics," *Journal of College Student Development* 57, no. 1 (January 2016): 104–9, https://doi.org/10.1353/csd.2016.0012.
10. Nancy O'Neill, "Internships as a High-Impact Practice: Some Reflections on Quality," *Peer Review* 12, no. 4 (Fall 2010), www.aacu.org/publications-research/periodicals/internships-high-impact-practice-some-reflections-quality; G. D. Kuh, *High-Impact Educational Practices: What They Are, Who Has Access to Them, and Why They Matter* (Washington, DC: Association of American Colleges & Universities, 2008), www.aacu.org/node/4084.

11. O'Neill, "Internships as a High-Impact Practice."
12. M. G. Kopp, "Internships in Special Collections: Experiential Pedagogy, Intentional Design, and High-Impact Practice," *Internships in Special Collections* 20, no. 1 (2019), 12–27.
13. Elizabeth M. Lee and Jacob Harris, "Counterspaces, Counterstructures: Low-Income, First-Generation, and Working-Class Students' Peer Support at Selective Colleges," *Sociological Forum* 35, no. 4 (2020): 1135–56, https://doi.org/10.1111/socf.12641.
14. Candice Dahl, "Creating Undergraduate Internships for Non-LIS Students in Academic Libraries," *Collaborative Librarianship* 3, no. 2 (2001): 73–78, https://doi.org/10.29087/2011.3.2.04.
15. Dahl, "Creating Undergraduate Internships."
16. Dahl, "Creating Undergraduate Internships."

About the Editor and Contributors

Sigrid Kelsey is director of scholarly publications at Louisiana State University. An award-winning librarian, she has coedited five books and written numerous articles. Kelsey has served on the ALA Publishing Committee and the American Libraries editorial advisory board. She is currently on the editorial board of Library Diversity and Residency Studies and is the general editor of *Catholic Library World*.

Kristina Clement is the student outreach and sponsored programs librarian at Kennesaw State University, and formerly the student success librarian at the University of Wyoming. She regularly works with transfer students, first-generation students, veterans, and other nontraditional populations to help them find their home in the library. Clement has often presented and published about universal design for learning in library instruction, outreach to transfer students and first-generation students, instructional assessment, and information privilege.

Jason Coleman is the head of library user services and an associate professor at the Kansas State University Libraries. Previously he was an undergraduate and community services librarian, a position in which he coordinated the University Libraries' general reference services. He holds an MLS from Emporia State University. He has held leadership positions on several committees in ALA's Reference and User Services Division and is a member of Kansas State University's JED Campus Team, a group dedicated to enhancing the university's mental health and wellness services.

Michelle R. Desilets is the education and science librarian at Portland State University (PSU). Her areas of interest include information literacy instruction, student research practices, online teaching and learning, and educational technology. She has presented and published on several of these topics, including her most recent article, "Accidental Information Literacy Instruction: The Work a Link Landing Page Can Do," in *Scholarship of Teaching and Learning, Innovative Pedagogy*. She is currently collaborating with colleague and coauthor Elizabeth Pickard on a study that examines the research practices of PSU geography majors.

Shannon Dew is the director of online library services at Florida State College at Jacksonville (FSCJ). She previously served as an associate dean and adjunct faculty member at FSCJ. She earned an MLIS degree from the University of Arizona. In her current role, she participates in the strategic planning of the Library and Learning Commons and has oversight of online library services, which includes management of the library's web presence, database resources, and OER collaboration.

Rosalind Fielder-Giscombe has been an associate professor of library and information services and a reference and instruction librarian at the Gwendolyn Brooks Library at Chicago State University since 2009. Her publications include a book chapter with Brandon C. Taylor in *Real-Life Distance Education: Cases in Practice*. She recently copresented a webinar entitled "Research Consultations as a Research Support in the Virtual Environment." She has served on committees in the Distance and Online Learning Section of the Association of College & Research Libraries.

Joyce Garczynski is the assistant university librarian for development and communications at Towson University's Albert S. Cook Library (in Maryland). In this role she teaches journalism students about the research process, manages her library's social media, and oversees the library's Data Studio. She obtained her MLS degree from the University of Maryland, College Park, and also has a master's degree in communication from the Annenberg School at the University of Pennsylvania.

ABOUT THE EDITOR AND CONTRIBUTORS / 185

Deborah Gaspar is the director of user services and collections at the Campbell Library of Rowan University (in Glassboro, New Jersey). She began her career in academic libraries at George Washington University, first as an instruction librarian and later as the instruction coordinator. In each of these roles, collaboration with student services and the Writing Center has been essential to delivering library teaching and learning to patrons. Gaspar earned her MLS at Drexel University and an EdD degree at St. Joseph's University.

Narcissa Haskins is the teaching and learning librarian at Louisiana State University, where she delivers instruction to undergraduate and general education students. She received her BA from Bennett College and her MLIS degree from the University of North Carolina at Greensboro. Haskins's varied work experiences have enhanced her life and passion for the multifaceted field of librarianship. Her interests include instructional design, community outreach, programming, and videography.

Karina Kletscher is the reference and instruction librarian at Creighton University. Her research interests include critical pedagogies and the intersection of information literacy and cultural programming and its impact on belonging in the academic library. She has previously written and presented on gamified library instruction, family spaces in the academic library, and librarians' roles in adolescent sexual health literacy. Kletscher has a BA from the University of Southern California and an MLIS degree from the University of Maryland, College Park.

Rachel Koszalka has lived and worked in rural Kansas communities her entire life and is the adult basic education instructor for Neosho County Community College. Based out of Independence, Kansas, she assists both traditional and nontraditional students in attaining their GEDs so they can achieve their personal and professional goals. She has an MLIS degree from Emporia State University and has previously worked with teens as the young adult programming librarian at the Coffeyville Public Library in Coffeyville, Kansas.

186 / ABOUT THE EDITOR AND CONTRIBUTORS

Leo S. Lo is the dean of college of university libraries and learning sciences at the University of New Mexico. Previously, he was associate dean for learning, undergraduate services, and commonwealth campus libraries at Pennsylvania State University. Lo holds an EdD degree in higher education management from the University of Pennsylvania, an MA in survey research from the University of Connecticut, an MSLS from Florida State University, an MFA in screenwriting from Hollins University, and a BA from the University of Texas at Arlington.

Jennifer Matthews is the collection strategy librarian at Rowan University (in Glassboro, New Jersey). In her current role she manages contracts, the library budget and acquisitions, assesses the library collections, and works closely with the library's vendors. She has written and presented research in the area of acquisitions and electronic resources issues, including open access initiatives, at various conferences and symposia.

Ebony McDonald is the African and African-American studies diversity librarian and first participant in the Diversity Residency Program at Louisiana State University Libraries in Baton Rouge, Louisiana. Prior to this role, she was the research and learning librarian at Salem College Libraries in Winston-Salem, North Carolina. At these institutions, McDonald has further developed her emerging expertise in library communications, information literacy instruction, and outreach and engagement.

Gretchen Mitchell is the deputy director of support services at the Jacksonville Public Library in Florida. She has worked in a variety of public and support positions during her tenure there. Her current role encompasses the facilities, finance, collection and cataloging management, integrated library system, and technology services for all twenty-one Jacksonville Public Library locations.

Susan Mythen is the director of campus library services at Florida State College at Jacksonville and is an adjunct professor in the University of Maryland Global Campus's First-Year Experience program. Her research has focused on collection management in community college libraries. She is the 2021–22 president of the ALA's Library Instruction Round Table.

About the Editor and Contributors

Lis Pankl is currently dean of libraries and a professor at Mississippi State University. She holds a PhD in geography from Kansas State University, an MPA from the University of Utah, an MSLS from the University of North Texas, an MA in English from Abilene Christian University, and a BA from Washington State University. Her areas of interest include higher education administration, organizational development, strategic planning, academic libraries, and critical/cultural geographies.

Elizabeth Pickard is the science and social sciences librarian at Portland State University. She served as coprincipal investigator on the LSTA-funded project "Ethnographic Research in Illinois Academic Libraries," and received a PSU Faculty Development grant for her study of geography majors' research practices. Pickard has authored multiple articles on library instruction and the research process in *Collaborative Librarianship* and other journals.

Michelle Reale is a professor and access services and outreach librarian at Arcadia University (in Glenside, Pennsylvania). She is the author of seven ALA monographs, including *Mentoring and Managing Students in the Academic Library* (2013).

Sarah Simms is the undergraduate and student success librarian at Louisiana State University. In this position, she is able to share her love of instruction, information literacy, and supporting student success through campus-wide collaborations focused on the first- and second-year curriculum. She has written and presented on social justice practices within libraries and the classroom, as well as the efficacy of librarian-led instruction.

Felicia A. Smith is the inaugural racial equality and social equity librarian at Stanford University. She created a paid summer internship for low-income, first-generation minority students and will relaunch this internship in 2022. She has presented at national and international conferences and has published peer-reviewed articles as well as a book, *Cybrarian Extraordinaire*. Smith previously worked as a criminal defense private investigator in Chicago, specializing in homicide and narcotics and carrying a .357 magnum revolver.

Tariana Smith is the reference librarian at Southern University at New Orleans. She is working on a doctorate of education in organizational change and leadership through Baylor University, focusing on developing change agents from a cultural perspective through diversity, inclusion, access, and best strategies or practices. She also provides training, support, and advocacy for open education resources and affordable learning.

Paizha Stoothoff is senior grant writer at HealthRIGHT 360, a nonprofit organization that provides integrated medical and behavioral health care services to low-income Californians. Her academic experience includes working as a humanities librarian at CSU Los Angeles from 2019 to 2021, as well as teaching grant-writing and English composition courses. She is interested in providing English students with professional development experiences that connect with their studies and open doors after graduation. She has a BA from CSU Long Beach, an MA in English from San Francisco State University, and an MLIS from San Jose State University.

Jenn Tirrell is the instruction and assessment librarian at Soka University of America (in Aliso Viejo, California). Her areas of interest are information literacy instruction, inclusive reference and library services, and creating engaging academic library spaces. She has a BA from the University of Massachusetts Amherst and an MLIS from the University of California, Los Angeles.

Gabrielle M. Toth has been a reference and instruction librarian at the Gwendolyn Brooks Library (GBL) at Chicago State University since 2005. She is currently the coordinator of reference services and has served as coordinator of the GBL's federal and state depository library collections since 2008. Toth is an associate professor of library and instruction services and served as that department's faculty chair, an elected position, from 2013 to 2020. She is also cochair of the University Accreditation Steering Committee and a member of the university's Student Success Task Force.

Heather VanDyne is the online learning librarian at Fort Hays State University in Hays, Kansas. She is also an adjunct newspaper instructor and a former children's librarian. She has worked in rural academic and public libraries in the southeastern Kansas area since 2016 doing school outreach, instruction, and programming that promotes information literacy, DEI, and cultural awareness.

Zara T. Wilkinson joined Rutgers University Libraries in 2012 as a reference and instruction librarian at the Paul Robeson Library. She is the subject librarian for the departments of education, English and communication, philosophy and religion, and visual, media, and performing arts at Rutgers University-Camden. She also serves on the team that oversees the open and affordable textbooks program.

Jonathan Wilson is the online/distant education librarian and coordinator at the Sherrod Library of East Tennessee State University. In this position he provides library resources for faculty, staff, and students, and teaches library instruction classes and serves as the personal librarian. Wilson was previously a student engagement and instruction specialist at the Sherrod Library. He holds a bachelor's degree in social work from East Tennessee State University and a master's degree in information sciences from the University of Tennessee.

Index

A
academic coaching, 64–65
academic integration, 54
academic libraries
   access to information, 99
   inclusive programming, 93–101
   laptop-lending programs of, 160
   LSU Libraries, support of research course, 37–47
   rural community college students and, 27–34
   student well-being and, 103–110
academic support services, 64, 65
access
   inclusive programming and, 99, 101
   information privilege and, 71
   See also digital divide; internet access
accessibility
   of library for students, 33–34
   rural community college students and, 27–34
   virtual access to libraries during pandemic, 29–30
ACRL
   See Association of College and Research Libraries
ACT, 45–46
ACT UP technique, 45
Adaptive Technology Center, 100
Adichie, Chimamanda Ngozi, 121
admissions
   to Chicago State University, 52
   to colleges, COVID-19 pandemic and, 45–46

   holistic admissions approach of LSU, 37–38
   Portland State University and, 18
AER (affordable educational resources), 99
Affordability Task Force, 61–62
affordable educational resources (AER), 99
Affordable Learning LOUISiana Initiative, 99
"Aflame and Unafraid: A Case Study on Creating Interactive Programming in Remote Learning" (Kletscher & Tirrell), 81–91
"Aflame and Unafraid" series
   assessment of, 88
   challenges of, 89
   Community Dialogues event, 85–87
   conclusion about, 90–91
   creation process, 83–84
   idea for, 82
   Planning Committee for, 83
   program description, 84–85
African Americans
   COVID-19 pandemic, impact on students, ix–x, 105
   diversity of college applicants, 46
   at Rowan University, 61
   student success, library support of, 54
   vulnerable students at CSU, 51–52
Albert S. Cook Library, 4–11
Albertson's Library at Boise State University, 106–107
Allen Community College, 28–34

American College Health Association
  on help for students with online
    learning, 32
  on students affected by pandemic,
    ix–x
anxiety, 39–40
Appalachia, 149–158
Appalachian Regional Commission
  (ARC), 150
Applied Social Research Lab, ETSU, 150
Arch, Xan, 74
Arlain, Mandissa, 160
art exhibition, 87, 89
ArtSteps
  challenges of, 89
  for SUA event series, 84, 90
Asian Americans, ix–x, 105
assessment, 88
asset-based instruction model, 46
assistance, 76
Association of American Colleges &
  Universities, 120
Association of College and Research
  Libraries (ACRL)
  *Framework for Informational Literacy
    for Higher Education*, 43
  STEM curricula, call for, 16
  on student well-being, 106
Astin, Alexander W., 53–54
Authoring Award, 142–143
autism, 99–100
Aviles, Jose, 38

B

Bandura, Albert, 15
Barbuti, Sandra, 14
Barchi, Robert, 137–138
barriers
  financial barriers of students, 152
  identification of, 97–98
  removal of, 98, 160
belief, 15
Bell, S., 65
belonging
  employment of students and, 119–120
  in first-generation STEM students,
    14, 15

ILI's impact on, 22
space/place for, 96–97
student success and, 53–55
virtual research consultations, survey
  responses, 57
best practices, for student internships,
  173
Bettencourt, Genia M., 14
Biology, Environmental Science and
  Management (ESM) classes, 17–21
BIPOC (Black, Indigenous, and People of
  Color) students, 108–109
Bischof, Chris, 126
Booth, Char, 71
branding, 9
"Bridging the Digital Divide in
  Appalachia" (Wilson), 149–158
broadband
  COVID-19 pandemic and access to,
    139
  digital divide in Wyoming, 71–72
  ETSU students, lack of access to, 150
  for rural areas, 29–30
Bruce, Symphony, 54, 55

C

California State University at Northridge
  Library, 107
California State University, Los Angeles
  (Cal State LA)
  background of, 171–172
  conclusion about, 180–181
  internships, literature review, 172–174
  internships/student assistantships,
    comparison of, 178–179
  library interns, 176–177
  paid positions for students, discussion
    of, 177, 180
  student assistants (digitization
    assistants), 174–175
Campbell Library (Rowan University
  Library), 61, 64–67
CARES Act
  ETSU technology funded by, 151, 152,
    153
  funding for FSCJ programs, 159, 162
Carr, Frank, 126–127

Center for Community College Student Engagement, 29
change
    COVID-19 pandemic, rapid changes with, 27–28
    ILI sessions for vulnerable students, 21
cheating, 30, 31
Chicago State University (CSU)
    student success, literature review, 53–55
    support of students as remote learners, 55–58
    vulnerable students, COVID-19 pandemic and, 51–53
Chronicle of Higher Education, 106
circulation
    laptop lending agreement, 165
    of laptops in FSCJ program, 162–163, 166
class discussion, 40–41
Clayton, Christine D., 63
Clement, Kristina
    information about, 183
    "Information Privilege and First-Generation Students," 71–79
    programming that fosters inclusion, xii
CMSRU (Cooper Medical School of Rowan University) Library, 61
Coleman, Jason
    information about, 183
    programming that fosters inclusion, xii
    on student well-being/libraries, 103–110
collaboration
    for "HSS 1000: Introduction to Research" course, 38–39
    for paid work experiences, 171, 172
    student success partnerships, 64–67
    See also partnerships
The Collaborative Imperative (Raspa & Ward), 65
collective inquiry, 63
College Board, 45–46
College of Communication and Information, 99–100
College of Humanities and Social Sciences (HSS), 37–47
College of William & Mary, 104
College Pulse, 29
college students
    research process for first-semester students at LSU, 37–47
    textbook affordability and, 135–143
    well-being of, 103–110
    See also students
communication
    for FSCJ laptop-lending program, 166–167
    for planning SUA event series, 83
    with students in online learning, 30–31
community colleges, rural, 27–34
Community Dialogues event
    description of, 85–87
    survey responses about, 88
computers
    CSU students, online learning challenges, 52
    for data-related makerspace, 6
    ETSU students without access to, 150
    ETSU's laptop-lending program, 151–153
    laptops for students at FSCJ, 159–168
concept mapping, 42
continuous learning, 63
Cook-Sather, Alison
    on belonging, 119
    on ethic of care, 120
    on opportunities for students, 121
Cooper Medical School of Rowan University (CMSRU) Library, 61
COVID-19 pandemic
    Cal State LA library interns and, 176, 177
    Cook Library's Data Studio and, 9, 10–11
    data divide and, 3
    economic impact on students, 143
    ETSU's response to technology needs of students, 149, 157

FSCJ's switch to remote learning, 159
impact on students, ix–x, 27–28
Librarian-In-Residence program and, 78, 79
LSU Libraries, teaching during pandemic, 44–45
OAT program and, 140–143
Rowan University and, 61–62
Rowan University Libraries and, 62–64, 67
rural community college challenges during, 29–30, 31–34
Soka University of America and, 81
student well-being and, 109, 110
support of students during, x–xi, 51–52
"Talk Back Sessions" during, 96–97
textbook affordability and, 135, 138–140
well-being crisis among students and, 104–106
critical pedagogy, 95–96
critical thinking, 43–44
Cuddapah, Jennifer L., 63
cultural capital, 94–95, 100

D

Dahl, Candice, 177
Daisaku and Kaneko Ikeda Library
"Aflame and Unafraid" series, 84–85
background/context, 82
challenges of series/exhibition, 89
Community Dialogues event, 85–87
Community Dialogues event, assessment of, 88
event series, conclusion about, 90–91
event series, future considerations, 90
event series, process for creating, 83–84
mission of, 81–82
Planning Committee, 83
virtual exhibition/opening party, 87
Damasco, Ione T., 109
data analysis and visualization competition, 10, 11
data divide, 3–11
data makerspace, 4–11

data skills
importance of, 3
makerspace at Albert S. Cook Library for, 4–11
Data Studio, Albert S. Cook Library, 4–11
degrees, 14
DEI (diversity, equity, and inclusion), 142, 143
DEIA (diversity, equity, inclusion, and anti-racism), 108
Desilets, Michelle R.
information about, 184
STEM courses at Portland State University, xi
on STEM librarianship, 13–22
Dew, Shannon
information about, 184
"Laptops for Students: An Academic and Public Library Partnership," 159–168
support of students, xiii
dialogues
about research, 40
in "Aflame and Unafraid" series, 82
Community Dialogues event, 85–87, 88
Reckoning Initiative for, 95
students, awareness of needs of, 93–94
digital divide
COVID-19 pandemic and, 139
data makerspace and, 4–11
ETSU's address of, 149–158
FSCJ students and, 160
information privilege and, 71–72
digitization, 174–175
disability services, 99–100
disenfranchised students, 115–121
diversity
of college applicants, 46
cultural capital, multiculturalism, critical pedagogy, 94–96
diverse students, support of, 94
economic stratification of students and, 61
diversity, equity, and inclusion (DEI), 142, 143

diversity, equity, inclusion, and anti-racism (DEIA), 108
Duc Bo Massey, Melanie, 108
DuFour, R., 63
Dunnington, Angela, 160

E

East Tennessee State University (ETSU)
  Lending Technology & Personal Librarian Program, 151–158
  personal librarian services, 156–157
  remote instruction, switch to, 149–150
Eastside College Preparatory School, 125–133
economic stratification, 61
Education Trust, 3–4
educators
  See faculty
emergency plan, 34
emergency preparedness, 33–34
emotions
  mind-mapping and, 42
  warmth-based instruction and, 39–41
empathy
  cultural capital of students and, 95
  for inclusive programming, 100, 101
  for interns, 132
  for internship, 131
  for students, 93–94
  support of students, 97
"Employing the Disenfranchised Student for Mentoring and Empowerment" (Reale), 115–121
employment
  COVID-19 pandemic and, 139–140
  employing disenfranchised student for mentoring/empowerment, 115–121
  paid positions for students at Cal State LA, 171–181
  Stanford University Library's paid summer internships, 125–133
empowerment, 115–121
Eng, S., 65
English Department, Cal State LA
  collaboration with University Library, 172

library interns, funding for, 176
student assistants, recruitment of, 175
enrichment activities, 128
ethic of care, 120
ETSU
  See East Tennessee State University
event series
  "Aflame and Unafraid" series, 84–85
  assessment of, 88
  challenges of, 89
  Community Dialogues event, 85–87
  conclusion about, 90–91
  idea of, 82
  Planning Committee for, 83
  process of, 83–84
  virtual exhibition/opening party, 87
exceptionality (disability) services, 99–100
exhibition
  for "Aflame and Unafraid" event series, 84, 87
  ArtSteps for SUA event series, 84
  for SUA event series, challenges of, 89

F

faculty
  COVID-19 pandemic, rapid changes with, 27–28
  FSCJ laptop-lending program, marketing to, 161–162
  ILI outreach, success of, 20–21
  ILI sessions at PSU and, 20
  new service models for research assistance, 55–57
  OAT program and, 138, 140–143
  remote learning via library workshops, 62–64
  rural community colleges survey, 30–34
  STEM faculty, 16, 20, 21
  student sense of belonging and, 54, 119
  textbook affordability and, 135, 137
faculty learning communities (FLC), 63
FAFSA (Free Application for Federal Student Aid), 28, 161
fear, 39–40

Federal Communications Commission, 72
fees, 129–130
Felten, Peter, 119, 120
field trips, 129
Fielder-Giscombe, Rosalind
  information about, 184
  on support of CSU students, 51–58
  work of, xi
financial aid
  FSCJ laptop program and, 161, 167
  for FSCJ students, 160
  number of students applying for, 28
financial difficulties
  of ETSU students, 150, 157
  of interns, 130, 131
financial support
  ETSU's address of digital divide, 149–158
  laptops for students at FSCJ, 159–168
  libraries providing, xii–xiii
  paid positions for students, 171–181
  Stanford University Library's paid summer internships, 125–133
  textbook affordability initiatives, 135–143
First-Gen and/or Low Income (FLI) Office staff, 131
First Gen Scholars program, 74, 75
first-generation students
  of Cal State LA, 171–172
  ILI integration into STEM courses, 13–14
  library outreach to, 73–74
  paid positions at Cal State LA for, 174
  paid summer internships for, 125–133
  textbook affordability and, 136
  at University of Wyoming, 72
first-semester students, 37–47
FLC (faculty learning communities), 63
Flexible Degree initiative, PSU, 17–19
Florida State College at Jacksonville (FSCJ)
  background of, 159–160
  CARES Act funding for, 159
  college laptop-lending program, 161–168

Florida State College of Jacksonville Foundation (FSCJF), 164–167
Florida State University's Project PALS, 99–100
Florida Virtual Campus students, 136
Floyd, George, 95, 110, 133
flyer, 76–77
food, 131, 132
Framework for Informational Literacy for Higher Education (ACRL), 43
Free Application for Federal Student Aid (FAFSA), 28, 161
Fruitvale Station (movie), 132–133
FSCJ
  See Florida State College at Jacksonville
full-time equivalent (FTE) enrollments, 52
funding
  for data makerspace, 7–8
  for FSCJ programs, 159
  for Lending Technology & Personal Librarian Program, 152
  for library interns, 176
  for makerspace, 4–5
  for OAT program, 142
  for paid internship program, 127
furniture, 7

G

Garczynski, Joyce
  information about, 184
  on makerspace at Towson University's Albert S. Cook Library, 3–11
  makerspace developed by, xi
Gaspar, Deborah
  information about, 185
  Rowan University, reenvisioning learning at, 61–67
  work of, xi
GBL (Gwendolyn Brooks Library), 51–58
Geography, Geology, and Systems Science classes, 17–19, 21
George Mason University, 106
George Washington University, 106
Georgia Piedmont Technical College, 160
Gerlich, Bella Karr, 117

Gilman, Isaac, 74
Glassdoor, 3
global citizenship, 81
Gold, H. E., 98
Gorman, Amanda
   "Aflame and Unafraid" series, 84–85
   Community Dialogues event, 85–87
   "The Hill We Climb," 82
   LibGuide for SUA event series, 83
   SUA event series, assessment of, 88
GoToMeeting, 56
graduation rates, 136
Griego, Adan, 130, 133
Gwendolyn Brooks Library (GBL), 51–58

H

Haskins, Narcissa
   connections with students, xi
   information about, 185
   on LSU Libraries' support of research course, 37–47
Hausmann, Leslie R. M., 54
Healthy Minds Study, Fall 2020, 104–105
Higgins, Silke, 30
high school students
   COVID-19 pandemic, rapid changes with, 27–28
   paid summer internships for, 125–133
higher education
   textbook affordability initiatives, 135–143
   university enrollment, decline in, 171–172
high-impact practices
   student employment and, 120
   in student internships, 173, 181
"The Hill We Climb" (Gorman)
   "Aflame and Unafraid" series, 82, 84–85
   Community Dialogues event, 85–87
   Gorman's delivery of, 87
Hispanics
   See Latinos
holistic admissions approach, 37
Holloway, Jonathan, 142
hotspots
   See internet hotspots

"HSS 1000: Introduction to Research" course, 37–47
HSS Residential College
   partnership with HSS librarian team, 39, 47
   teaching during COVID-19 pandemic, 44–45
humanities, 171, 172

I

IDEA (Inclusion, Diversity, Equity, and Accessibility) Council, 98
"Identifying and Addressing the Evolving Accessibility Limitations of Rural Community College Students" (VanDyne & Koszalka), 27–34
ILI
   See information literacy instruction
Illinois Board of Higher Education, 52
inclusion
   employing disenfranchised students, 115–121
   inclusive programming, 93–101
   information privilege/first-generation students, 71–79
   interactive programming in remote learning at SUA, 81–91
   programming that fosters, xi–xii
Inclusion, Diversity, Equity, and Accessibility (IDEA) Council, 98
inclusive programming
   of academic libraries, 93
   access, 99
   barriers, identification of, 97–98
   barriers, removal of, 98
   conclusion about, 100–101
   cultural capital, multiculturalism, critical pedagogy, 94–96
   empathy, 93–94
   exceptionality (disability) services, 99–100
   relatedness/belonging, 96–97
   support of students, 94, 97
"Inclusive Programming" (Smith), 93–101
Independence Community College, 32

information literacy instruction (ILI)
    active learning, 43–44
    conclusion about/future research, 21–22
    for first-generation STEM students, 14–16
    ILI sessions, case findings, 17–19
    ILI sessions, impact of, 19–20
    integration into STEM courses, 13–14
    mind-mapping and, 40–43
    outreach opportunities, 20–21
    targeted services to vulnerable students, 21
    warmth-based instruction, 39–40
Information Literacy Standards for Science and Engineering/Technology (ACRL), 16
information privilege
    definition of, 71
    first-generation students at University of Wyoming and, 72, 78, 79
    invisible knapsack illustration, 73
    "Information Privilege and First-Generation Students" (Clement), 71–79
information timeline, 42
INROADS, 126–127
Inside Higher Ed
    on first-generation STEM students, 13
    on support for first-generation students, 14
    survey of student experiences, 29
internet access
    CSU students, online learning challenges, 52
    digital divide in Wyoming, 71–72
    ETSU's address of digital divide, 149–158
    FSCJ students and, 160
    for online learning, 29
    for rural community college students, 31–32
internet hotspots
    cost of, 158
    ETSU's provision of, 151, 152
    Lending Technology Program, impact of, 154–156

internship, Stanford University Libraries
    background of, 125–126
    conclusion about, 132–133
    lessons learned, 129–132
    logistics of, 126–129
internships
    library interns, 176–177
    literature review, 172–174
    mentorship in, 180
    paid summer internships, 125–133
    pros/cons of, 177, 178–179
interviews, 6
invisible knapsack, 72, 73

J

Jackson, Jennifer M., 107
Jacksonville, Florida, 160
Jacksonville Public Library (JPL)
    feedback on JPL-FSCJ laptop project, 167
    partnership for laptop-lending program, 164–167
JED Foundation, 105
jobs
    See employment

K

Kansas, rural community college survey, 28–34
Kansas Office of Rural Prosperity, 29–30
Kansas State University Libraries, 107
Kelsey, Sigrid
    information about, 183
    introduction by, ix–xiii
Kendrick, Kaetrena Davis, 30, 109
Kletscher, Karina
    information about, 185
    on interactive programming in remote learning, 81–91
    programming that fosters inclusion, xii
Kopp, M. G., 173
Koszalka, Rachel
    on accessibility limitations of rural college students, 27–34
    information about, 185
    on rural community college students, xi

Kuh, George D., 120

L
laptop-lending program
  of academic libraries, 160
  conclusion about, 168
  criteria for, 161
  discussion/analysis of, 167–168
  ETSU's purchase of laptops, 152
  FSCJ, background of, 159–160
  funding for, 159
  initial circulation data, 162–163
  marketing to students/faculty, 161–162
  public library partnership for, 164–167
"Laptops for Students: An Academic and Public Library Partnership" (Dew, Mitchell, & Mythen), 159–168
Latinos
  at Chicago State University, 52
  COVID-19 pandemic, impact on students, ix–x
  diversity of college applicants, 46
  at Rowan University, 61
  student success, library support of, 54
Lending Technology & Personal Librarian Program, ETSU
  beginning of, 151–152
  conclusion about, 157–158
  impact of, 154–156
  implementation of, 152–154
  personal librarian services, 156–157
lessons learned
  from paid summer internships, 129–132
  from SUA event series, 81, 108–109
LibChat, 56
LibGuide
  for FSCJ laptop-lending program, 162
  for SUA event series, 83–84, 87
  of UW Libraries, 77
Librarian-In-Residence program
  assistance/publicity, 76–77
  frequency, duration, access, location, 75–76
  LibGuide and, 77
  outcomes of, 78–79
  participation in, 75
librarians
  COVID-19 pandemic, rapid changes with, 27–28
  cultural capital, multiculturalism, critical pedagogy, 94–96
  diverse students, support of, 94
  empathy towards students, 93–94
  employment of students and, 115–121
  ETSU's personal librarian services, 156–157
  GBL, support of students as remote learners, 51–58
  ILI sessions for STEM courses at PSU, 17–22
  Librarian-In-Residence program of UW Libraries, 75–79
  paid positions for students and, 171–181
  on Planning Committee for SUA event series, 83
  remote learning via library workshops, 62–64
  research assistance, new service models for, 55–57
  research process for first-semester students at LSU, 37–47
  rural community colleges survey, 30–34
  virtual research consultations, survey responses, 57–58
librarianship, 180
See also STEM librarianship
libraries
  COVID-19 pandemic, rapid changes with, 27–28
  emergency preparedness of, 33–34
  employing disenfranchised student for mentoring/empowerment, 115–121
  financial support from, xii–xiii
  inclusive programming, 93–101
  library outreach to first-generation students, 73–74
  partnership for FSCJ laptop-lending program, 164–167

partnership for FSCJ laptop-lending *(continued)*
  relatedness/belonging, space for, 96–97
  student access to during pandemic, 29–30
  student well-being and, 103–110
  support of student learning, ix–xiii
  textbook affordability crisis, response to, 136–137
  well-being crisis, response to, 106–108
library interns
  at Cal State LA Library, 176–177
  mentorship for, 180
  pros/cons of position, 177, 178–179
Library Journal, 13
library resources, 43–44
library workshops
  remote learning via, 62–64
  of Rowan University Libraries, 65–67
literature review
  on first-generation STEM students, 14–16
  on internships, 172–174
  on student success, 53–55
Lo, Leo S.
  information about, 186
  programming that fosters inclusion, xii
  on student well-being/libraries, 103–110
Louisiana Library Network, 99
Louisiana State University (LSU)
  CARES Act funding for equipment, 152
  research process for first-semester students at, 37–47
Louisiana State University (LSU) Libraries
  diversity workshop of, 94
  relaxation room at, 107
  research process for first-semester students at, 37–47
"Loving Libraries" (Smith), 125–133
low-income students, 136
LSU
  See Louisiana State University

lunches, 131, 132
Lythcott-Haims, Julie, 132–133

M
Magi, Trina, 55
makerspace
  concept, refinement of, 5–7
  funding for, 7–8
  in future, 10–11
  idea for, 4–5
  promotion of, 8–10
Maloney, Krisellen, 142
Mardeusz, Patricia E., 55
marketing
  for "Aflame and Unafraid" event series, 85, 86
  of data makerspace, 8–10
  of FSCJ laptop-lending program, 161–162, 165–166
  for SUA event series, 89
  See also promotion
Matthews, Jennifer
  information about, 186
  Rowan University, reenvisioning learning at, 61–67
  work of, xi
McClusky, H. Y., 97
McDonald, Ebony
  connections with students, xi
  information about, 186
  on LSU Libraries' support of research course, 37–47
McIntosh, Peggy, 72
Mellon, C. A., 40
mental health, 104–106
mentoring
  employing students for, 115–121
  Felicia Smith as mentor, 127
  First Gen Scholars program, 74
Microsoft Office, 78
mind-mapping
  online mind map, 45
  for research course, 40–43
minority students
  paid summer internships for, 127–128
  at Rowan University, 61
  textbook affordability and, 136–137

textbook affordability/COVID-19 pandemic and, 139–140
vulnerable students at CSU, 51–52
well-being crisis among, 104–106
Mitchell, Gretchen
  information about, 186
  "Laptops for Students: An Academic and Public Library Partnership," 159–168
  support of students, xiii
Mitola, Rosan, 120
monetary compensation, 173–174
money, 130–132
Moreno, Teresa Helena, 107
motivation, of student workers, 117–118
MS Teams, 83
multiculturalism, 95, 100
Mythen, Susan B.
  information about, 186
  "Laptops for Students: An Academic and Public Library Partnership," 159–168
  support of students, xiii

N

National Center for Education Statistics, 13, 136
National Research Council, 16
Native Americans and Alaskan Natives
  COVID-19 pandemic, impact on students, ix–x, 105
  diversity of college applicants, 46
Native Hawaiians or Pacific Islanders, 105
NBC, 135
Neosho County Community College, 28–34
"Night Against Procrastination" program, 66
North Carolina State University Libraries, 107–108

O

OAT program
  See Open and Affordable Textbooks (OAT) program

obstacles
  for interns, 130–131
  for students, removal of, 98
  See also barriers
OER
  See open educational resources
Office of Academic Innovation (OAI), 17
Office of Diversity, Equity, and Inclusion, 83
O'Keefe, Patrick, 54
online learning
  ETSU's switch to, 149–150
  GBL, support of students as remote learners, 51–58
  LSU Libraries, teaching during pandemic, 44–45
  OAT program/COVID-19 pandemic, 140–143
  shift to, difficulties with, 30–32
  student experiences of, 29
  textbook affordability/COVID-19 pandemic and, 139–140
  See also remote learning
online resources, for student well-being, 110
open access content, 99
Open and Affordable Textbooks (OAT) program
  COVID-19 pandemic and, 140–143
  creation of, 137–138
  significance of, 135
  success of, 143
open educational resources (OER)
  access to, 99
  Rowan University Libraries and, 61–62
  Rutgers University Libraries and, 142–143
  textbook affordability crisis, response to, 137
open textbooks
  OAT program/COVID-19 pandemic and, 140–143
  textbook affordability crisis, response to, 137
Opening Party, 87
Ormrod, Jeanne Ellis, 96

Otto, Kate, 120
Otto, Megan, 107–108
outreach
    for ILI in STEM courses, 13–14, 16, 21–22
    ILI sessions, outreach for, 17–19
    library outreach to first-generation students, 73–74
    opportunities for ILI, 20–21

P

paid positions for students
    Cal State LA, background of, 171–172
    conclusion about, 180–181
    discussion of, 177, 180
    internships, literature review, 172–174
    internships/student assistantships, comparison of, 178–179
    library interns, 176177
    student assistants (digitization assistants), 174–175
"Paid Positions for Students: A Win-Win for Everyone Involved" (Stoothoff), 171–181
pandemic
    See COVID-19 pandemic
Pankl, Lis
    information about, 187
    programming that fosters inclusion, xii
    on student well-being/libraries, 103–110
partnerships
    for diversity training, 94
    for ETSU response to digital divide, 151
    faculty/Rowan Libraries partnership for library workshop, 62
    FSCJ/JPL partnership for laptop-lending program, 164–167
    student success partnerships, 64–67
    for student well-being services, 106–107
    See also collaboration
Pascarell, Rose, 104
peer-mentor program, 74
Penn State University, 107

Perry, Heather Brodie, 16
personal librarian (PL)
    for ETSU students, 151
    ETSU's personal librarian services, 156–157
Personal Librarian Program (PLP), 74–75
Peterson, Christine, 72
Phillips, Margaret, 15
Pickard, Elizabeth
    information about, 187
    STEM courses at Portland State University, xi
    on STEM librarianship, 13–22
Planning Committee, 83, 90
"Planning Your Semester" session, 66
PLM (power-load margin), 97
PLP (Personal Librarian Program), 74–75
Porte, Olivia, 121
Portland State University (PSU)
    ILI integration into STEM courses, 13–14
    ILI outreach efforts by librarians at, 17
    ILI sessions, case findings, 17–19
    ILI sessions, conclusion about, 21–22
    ILI sessions, impact of, 19–20
    outreach opportunities, taking advantage of, 20–21
    targeted services to vulnerable students under rapid change, 21
power-load margin (PLM), 97
"Prep for Finals!" session, 66–67
programming, xi–xii
    See also inclusive programming
Project ENABLE (Expanding Non-Discriminatory Access by Librarians Everywhere), 100
Project PALS, Florida State University, 99–100
Project to Recruit the Next Generation of Librarians internship, 127
promotion
    of data makerspace, 8–10
    of Lending Technology & Personal Librarian Program, 153–154
    of Librarian-In-Residence program, 76–77

of SUA event series, 89
  See also marketing
PSU
  See Portland State University

Q
question-and-answer knowledge checks, 44

R
race/ethnicity
  college graduation rates by, 136
  student success, campus involvement and, 54
  textbook affordability/COVID-19 pandemic and, 139–140
  well-being crisis among minoritized students, 104–106
racism, systemic
  resources for/support of students, 109
  student well-being, lessons learned, 108–109
  vulnerable students and, 105
Raspa, Dick, 65
Reale, Michelle
  "Employing the Disenfranchised Student for Mentoring and Empowerment," 115–121
  information about, 187
  programming that fosters inclusion, xii
Reckoning Initiative, 95
"Reenvisioning Learning in a Time of Disruption" (Matthews & Gaspar), 61–67
reference services
  GBL, live reference services during pandemic, 55–56
  virtual research consultations, 57–58
relatedness, 96–97
relationships
  for inclusive programming, 100
  between librarians/STEM faculty, 20, 21, 22
  online learning, instructor-student relationships, 30–31
  relatedness/belonging and, 96–97
  student/librarian relationships, 55
  support of students, 97
remote learning
  event series of SUA, 81–91
  FSCJ laptop-lending program for students, 161
  FSCJ's switch to, 159
  GBL, new service models for research assistance, 55–57
  GBL, support of students as remote learners, 51–58
  ILI sessions for vulnerable students, 21
  OAT program/COVID-19 pandemic, 140–143
  Rowan Libraries' library workshops, 62–64
  Rowan University Libraries, student success partnerships, 64–67
  support of students in rapidly changing learning environments, x–xi
  virtual research consultations, 57–58
  See also online learning
research
  "HSS 1000: Introduction to Research," LSU Libraries' support of, 37–47
  ILI sessions, case findings, 18–19
  new service models for research assistance, 55–57
  teaching styles/techniques for, 39–44
  virtual research consultations, 56–58
research consultations, 56–57
research guide, 44
Ric Edelman College of Communication and Creative Arts, 66–67
Rinto, Erin, 120
Roksa, Josipa, 108
Rowan School of Osteopathic Medicine (SOM) Health Sciences Library, 61
Rowan University, 61–67
Rowan University Libraries (RUL)
  COVID-19 pandemic and, 61–62
  remote learning via library workshops, 62–64
  student success partnerships, 64–67

transition to remote learning, conclusion about, 67
Rubalcava, Veronica, 130–132
rural community colleges
   accessibility for underserved students, 34
   challenges of rural community colleges, 29–30
   COVID-19 pandemic, rapid changes with, 27–28
   emergency preparedness, 33–34
   survey, research method/response, 30–33
Rutgers Biomedical and Health Sciences, 137
Rutgers Today, 142
Rutgers University
   COVID-19 pandemic and, 139–140
   OAT and COVID-19 pandemic, 140–143
   OAT program at, 137–138
   textbook affordability crisis and, 135
Rutgers University Libraries
   OAT program, 137–138
   OAT/COVID-19 pandemic, 140–143
Rutgers University-Camden, 137
Rutgers University-New Brunswick, 137
Rutgers University-Newark, 137
Ryerson University Library, 160

S
SAT, 45–46
scaffolding, 18–19, 39
scheduling, 85, 128
Schmelzer, Elise, 72
Schreiner, Laurie A., 53–54
self-efficacy
   ILI for support of, 14–16
   ILI's impact on, 22
   of students, removal of barriers and, 98
   support of students for, 97
sensitivity, 131, 132
service models, for research assistance, 55–57
Shaw, Emily J., 14
Sherrod Library, 152–154

Simms, Sarah
   connections with students, xi
   information about, 187
   on LSU Libraries' support of "HSS 1000: Introduction to Research," 37–47
Simpson, Bethany, 160
SIUE (Southern Illinois University at Edwardsville), 108, 109
"Small Victories in STEM Librarianship" (Pickard & Desilets), 13–22
smartphones
   for internet access, 160
   student use of for online coursework, 150
Smith, Felicia A.
   information about, 187
   library internships, xii
   on Stanford University Library's paid summer internships, 125–133
Smith, Tariana
   on inclusive programming, xii, 93–101
   information about, 188
"So Close and Yet So Remote" (Fielder-Giscombe & Toth), 51–58
social class, 54
social justice
   in academic library programming, 81
   "Aflame and Unafraid" event series, 84–85, 87
   SUA event series, assessment of, 88
   SUA event series for, 82
Socratic method, 44
software, 8
Soka University of America (SUA)
   "Aflame and Unafraid" series, 84–85
   challenges of series/exhibition, 89
   Community Dialogues event, 85–87
   Community Dialogues event, assessment of, 88
   description of, 81
   event series, background/context, 82
   event series, conclusion about, 90–91
   event series, future considerations, 90
   event series, process for creating, 83–84
   mission of library, 81–82

Planning Committee, 83
virtual exhibition/opening party, 87
Southeastern Louisiana University
 Library, 160
Southeastern University, 100
Southern Illinois University at
 Edwardsville (SIUE), 108, 109
Southern University at New Orleans'
 Leonard S. Washington Memorial
 Library, 96–97
Stadler, D., 65
Stahura, Dawn, 45
Stanford University Libraries
 internship program, conclusion
  about, 132–133
 internship program, lessons learned,
  129–132
 internship program, logistics of,
  126–129
 partnership with Eastside College
  Preparatory School, 125–126
Stanford's Opportunity Fund, 131–132
Stanford's Virtual Human Interaction
 Lab, 129
Statement Magazine, 174–175
STEM librarianship
 background/methodology, 17
 case findings, 17–19
 conclusion about/future research,
  21–22
 ILI integration into STEM courses,
  13–14
 impact of, 19–20
 literature review, 14–16
 outreach opportunities, 20–21
 targeted services to vulnerable
  students, 21
stereotypes, 121
Stoothoff, Paizha
 information about, 188
 "Paid Positions for Students: A Win-
  Win for Everyone Involved,"
  171–181
 support of students, xiii
Strayhorn, Terrell L., 54, 119
student assistants (digitization
 assistants)

 at Cal State LA Library, 174–175
 mentorship for, 180
 pros/cons of position, 177, 178–179
student borrowing agreement, 166
student engagement, 117
Student Public Interest Research
 Groups, 136
student retention, 65
student success librarian, 75–79
student technology fees, 8
"Student Well-Being and Libraries"
 (Coleman, Pankl, & Lo), 103–110
students
 barriers, identification of, 97–98
 barriers, removal of, 98
 of Cal State LA, 171–172
 COVID-19 pandemic, impact on, 34,
  143
 cultural capital, multiculturalism,
  critical pedagogy, 94–96
 diverse students, support of, 94
 empathy for inclusive programming,
  93–94
 employing disenfranchised students,
  115–121
 ETSU's laptop-lending program,
  149–158
 event series of SUA and, 81–91
 first-generation STEM students, ILI
  for, 14–16
 first-generation students at University
  of Wyoming, 72
 GBL, support of students as remote
  learners, 51–58
 ILI integration into STEM courses,
  13–14
 inclusive programming for, 93–101
 internships, literature review, 172–174
 laptop-lending program, 161–163
 libraries' support of, ix–xiii
 library outreach to first-generation
  students, 73–74
 paid positions for students at Cal State
  LA, 171–181
 relatedness/belonging, 96–97
 remote learning via library
  workshops, 62–64

research process for first-semester students at LSU, 37–47
rural community college students, accessibility issues, 27–34
of Soka University of America, 81
Stanford University Library's paid summer internships, 125–133
student success, library/librarian roles in, 53–55
student success partnerships, 64–67
support of, 97
virtual research consultations, survey responses, 57–58
well-being, lessons learned about, 108–109
well-being crisis, academic libraries' response to, 106–108
well-being crisis among minoritized students, 104–106
well-being of, 103–110

SUA
See Soka University of America

success
library/librarian support of student success, 53–55
student success partnerships, 64–67
of students, virtual reference services and, 58

Summer Bridge Plus, 151
summer internships, 125–133

support
of diverse students, 94
for inclusive programming, 101
of student employees, 118
of students, x–xi, 97

survey
for ETSU students, 150
for FSCJ laptop-lending program, 161–162, 163
rural community college survey, 28–34
for SUA event series, 88
on virtual research consultations, 57–58

"Survey of Student Readiness in Online Learning" (FSCJ), 161–162
Syracuse University, 100

systemic racism
See racism, systemic

T

"Taking a Byte Out of the Data Divide" (Garczynski), 3–11
"Talk Back Sessions," 96–97
teaching styles/techniques, 39–44
technical support, 167–168
technology
digital divide, 139–140
ETSU's Lending Technology & Personal Librarian Program, 151–157
ETSU's purchase of, 152–153
funding for makerspace technology, 8
for inclusive programming, 100
laptop-lending programs, 160
library emergency preparedness and, 33–34
questions for makerspace creation, 6
tests, 45–46
textbook affordability
affordability crisis, 135–137
conclusion about, 143
COVID-19 pandemic and, 139–140
OAT/COVID-19 pandemic, 140–143
Open and Affordable Textbooks program at Rutgers University, 137–138
textbook revolution, 136–137
"theory of margin," 97
"Throwing the University Wide Open" (Wilkinson), 135–143
time, 20
Tinto, Vincent, 15
Tirrell, Jennifer
case study on interactive programming in remote learning, 81–91
information about, 188
programming that fosters inclusion, xii
Tobin House, University of Wyoming
creation of, 74
LibGuide and, 77

Librarian-In-Residence program, 75–77
Librarian-In-Residence program, outcomes of, 78–79
"Together from the Ground Up" (Simms, Haskins, & McDonald), 37–47
Toth, Gabrielle
  information about, 188
  on support of CSU students, 51–58
  work of, xi
Towson University, 4–11
training
  of interns, 128–129
  of student assistants, 175
Tran, Ngox-Yen, 30
transactional relationship, 120
TRiO program, 151
Tritt, Deborah, 30
tutoring
  personal librarian services, 156
  at Rowan University Libraries, 64, 65
Tysick, Cynthia, 41–42

U

Undergraduate Engagement Program, 107
underserved students
  COVID-19 pandemic, impact on, 34
  textbook affordability and, 136–137
understanding
  cultural capital of students and, 95
  for inclusive programming, 100
  of students, 93–94
University Libraries at the University of North Carolina at Chapel Hill (UNC), 98
University Library, Cal State LA, 172
University of California at Los Angeles, 137
University of California at San Diego Libraries, 108
University of California Berkeley Library, 106
University of Chicago, 107
University of Denver Libraries, 94
University of Massachusetts Amherst, 137
University of North Carolina at Chapel Hill, 95
University of Notre Dame, 127
University of Texas at Austin, 29
University of Wyoming
  digital divide in Wyoming, 71–72
  Librarian-in-Residence program at Tobin House, outcomes, 78–79
  library outreach to first-generation students, 73–74
  library support for first-generation students, 74–77
University of Wyoming Libraries
  digital divide in Wyoming, 71–72
  Librarian-in-Residence program at Tobin House, outcomes, 78–79
  library outreach to first-generation students, 73–74
  library support for first-generation students, 74–77
"Upgrade Your Grade" programs, 64, 65–67

V

VanDyne, Heather
  on accessibility limitations of rural college students, xi, 27–34
  information about, 189
video, 129
virtual exhibition
  for "Aflame and Unafraid" event series, 87
  ArtSteps for SUA event series, 84
  for SUA event series, 88, 89
virtual learning
  See online learning; remote learning
virtual programming
  as challenge of SUA event series, 89
  SUA event series, 81–91
virtual reality (VR), 84
virtual research consultations
  of GBL, 56–57
  response to, 57–58
vulnerable students
  at CSU, 51–52
  ILI sessions for, 21
  success of, support of, 53–55

vulnerable students *(continued)*
   support of, ix–x, 97
   well-being crisis among minoritized students, 104–106

W
Wang, Weina, 160
Ward, Dane, 65
warmth-based instruction, 39–41
Washington, Booker T., 125
web-conferencing software, 56
well-being
   conclusion about, 110
   crisis among minoritized students, 104–106
   lessons learned, 108–109
   of students, 103–110
Wellbeing Collaborative, 105
wellness, 104, 109
"Wellness Days," 107
Wenger, Etienne, 63
"White Privilege: Unpacking the Invisible Knapsack" (McIntosh), 72
Whitley, Sarah E., 108
Wi-Fi, 150
Wilkinson, Zara T.
   information about, 189
   open-textbook program, xii
   on textbook affordability, 135–143
Wilmoth, Wendy S., 160
Wilson, Jonathan Roy
   on ETSU's laptop-lending/personal librarian programs, 149–158
   information about, 189
   support of students, xiii
work
   See employment
work experience
   benefits of, 173–174
   high school students in library, 109
   paid positions for students, 171–181
   paid summer internships, 125–133
workshops, library, 62–64
Writing Center
   event series of SUA, 82
   Planning Committee for event series, 83
   at Rowan University Libraries, 64
   support of students, 65
writing specialists, 83
Wyoming, 71–72

Z
Zoom
   with librarians at GBL, 56
   for Rowan University Libraries workshops, 66
   rural community college students and, 31, 32
   for SUA event series, 89, 90
   for virtual research consultations, 56
Zwicky, Dave, 15